Emi
Entre
and
Evil Spirits

MW00640174

Emigrants, Entrepreneurs, and Evil Spirits

LIFE IN A PHILIPPINE VILLAGE

STEPHEN GRIFFITHS

A Kolowalu Book
UNIVERSITY OF HAWAII PRESS
Honolulu

© 1988 STEPHEN GRIFFITHS
ALL RIGHTS RESERVED
MANUFACTURED IN THE UNITED STATES OF AMERICA

Library of Congress Cataloging-in-Publication Data

Griffiths, Stephen L.
    Emigrants, entrepreneurs, and evil spirits: life in a Philippine
village/Stephen Griffiths.
        p.   cm.—(A Kolowalu book)
    Includes index.
    ISBN 0–8248–1156–9   ISBN 0–8248–1185–2 (pbk.)
    1. Ilokanos (Philippine people)—Social conditions.   2. Ilokanos
(Philippine people)—Commerce.   3. Ilokanos (Philippine people)—
Religion.   4. Ilocos Norte (Philippines)—Emigration and
immigration.   I. Title.
DS666.I37G75   1988   88–1319
306'.0899921—dc19   CIP

To my mother,
Ernestine Coles Griffiths

SPECIAL NOTE

Bawang is not the real name of the village where I conducted my research. A few other place names both in the Philippines and Hawaii are also fictitious. Furthermore, I have changed the names of all the villagers described in this book, including the members of my host family.

CONTENTS

ACKNOWLEDGMENTS

I am indebted to the people of Bawang, and especially to my host family, for having me as a guest in their village for the duration of my research. Villagers tolerated my inquisitiveness graciously, and I remember their company with pleasure.

My research in the Philippines was conducted while I was a graduate student in the Department of Anthropology at the University of Hawaii and was supported by a grant from the National Institute of Mental Health.

Several friends read and commented on earlier versions of this work, and I would like to thank them here: Roger Farrand, Charles Finklestein, Hans Hollitscher, Henry T. Lewis, Richard W. Lieban, Harold J. McArthur, Jr., Thomas Mitchell, Suzanne Ortiz, Suzanne Raftery, Marla Riley, Ruth Ann Sando, Alice Sim, and my aunt, Carey C. Perry.

I owe special thanks to Nancy Grant and Philip Preston for their editing skills, and to Nancy also for drawing the map in this book. I am grateful to George Winsley for the use of his printer.

At the University of Hawaii Press, I appreciate the advice I received from Iris Wiley, and I am grateful to Pamela Kelley, who edited the book, for the many excellent suggestions she made to improve it.

The responsibility for the content, of course, is entirely my own.

Emigrants,
Entrepreneurs,
and
Evil Spirits

Village of Bawang

Enrique Cruz

Berto Castro

Maximo Espiritu

Segundo + Mercedes Tolentino

Innocencio Valdez

Polycarpio Ramirez

FIESTA GROUNDS

Alberto Ruiz

Pasqual Gomez

RICE MILL

Rafael + Estrelita Solano

Wilfredo + Pura Castro

Diony Bautista

LAOAG

MANILA

Conrado Ventura

NEW POPULAR STORE

SIMBAAN RIVER

PAMIITAN (rain-fed rice fields)

BANGKAG ////// (vegetable gardens)

IRRIGATED RICE FIELDS

South China Sea

Ilocos Norte
o Laoag
o Simbaan
o Vigan
Abra
Ilocos Sur

o Manila

ncg

Introduction

"How would you like your eggs in the morning, Steve, sunnyside-up or over easy?" No anthropologist, I was sure, had ever been asked this question by a villager upon selecting a research site. I was delighted.

It was January of 1973, and I was in the province of Ilocos Norte in the Philippines for what would be the first of two anthropological field trips. I was interested in the changes that had occurred in a peasant village as a result of villagers migrating to Hawaii to work in the sugar plantations. Had the emigrants maintained close ties with their home communities? Had any returned and, if so, how had they readapted to life in the village after their sojourns abroad? For a nation of immigrants, Americans know little of the villages their ancestors left behind. I did not want this to be the case for the majority of Filipino-Americans who could trace their ancestry to the Ilocos region, a narrow strip of land along the northwest coast of the island of Luzon.

As I got on the bus that would take me to the city of Laoag where I had been staying for the past month, I gave Berto Castro, who had accompanied me to the roadside, my answer. Berto, now plump and bald, had gone to Hawaii as a young man in the 1930s and then moved on to California to work in the vineyards. He received a pension from the U.S. government, and he served as an elected village counselor. Along with officials from the nearby municipal town of Simbaan, he had introduced me to a family in the village who had agreed to accept me into their home for the duration of my research. My future hosts, Raphael and Estrelita Solano, were no doubt concerned about my eating habits, and Berto, familiar with the American diet, had taken the opportunity of inquiring for them.

"Thanks, Berto," I replied, "but a *pan-de-sal* [roll] and a cup of

1

coffee will be just fine." Berto looked a little disappointed, but I knew my hosts would be relieved: maybe I wouldn't be such a difficult houseguest after all.

This was not my first trip to the Philippines or to Ilocos Norte. In a sense, I was an emigrant returning for a visit myself. I had grown up in the Philippines where my parents served as Episcopalian missionaries, my father being a minister and educator. My first trip to Ilocos Norte took place in 1949 when I was three. I celebrated my birthday in the coastal resort of Banua. At the time my parents were serving at one of the most isolated mission stations on Luzon, the tiny village of Balbalasang in what is now the subprovince of Kalinga-Apayao, located deep in the forested mountains of the Cordillera Central. In need of a short vacation, my parents decided to leave the mountains and visit Banua for a few days. This entailed a full day's hike from Balbalasang to the road in Abra Province. Here a jeep met us for the drive to the lowlands. I remember becoming nauseated by the combination of great speed, exceptional humidity and heat, and columns of dust. We were visiting the Ilocos region at the peak of its long dry season.

When we reached the coast, we headed north, the China Sea glistening a deep blue on our left. To our right a few miles away, the Cordillera Central rose, a giant purple wall. Interrupted here and there by low-lying hills burned brown, the lowlands were divided into rice fields. Only a few of them were irrigated and in production. The rest were barren, their clay beds cracked into wide fissures. Occasionally, we crossed a river or stream. In the distance we could see villages along beaches and at the foot of hills. The houses were of thatch and bamboo. Every thirty kilometers or so we passed through a town. Each reflected its colonial Spanish heritage by a red brick church and tower and a large central plaza. Acacia and mango trees lined the streets, providing refreshing shade.

As we neared Banua, at the northernmost tip of Luzon where the mountains meet the sea, we found fewer towns. The resort was small, a single building with only four guestrooms and a dining room. A freshwater swimming pool was set in a nicely kept green lawn in front of the building. The sea lapped the rocky shore a short distance away. Drying seaweed and tidal pools gave the air a salty, pungent aroma.

I remember little of our few days' stay at Banua except the bright beach ball I received as a birthday gift, the oddness I felt at being immersed in cool, still water (I was used to daily "swims" in Balbalasang's Saltan River), and the hours spent hunting for seashells, most bleached lavender by the sun. I also remember the story my mother tells of my *amah* Theodora's reaction to seeing the sun set over the water for the first time. "Mrs. Griffiths," she called in alarm, "the sea is eating the sun!"

Initially, I had been reluctant to select a research site in the Philippines. Since I was being trained as an anthropologist, I thought that perhaps I should choose an unfamiliar country. But I was interested in the topic of emigration, in particular the changes that occur in the communities left behind. And the Philippines was a logical choice for a student in Hawaii like myself. Many Filipinos had moved to the Islands and more were coming each year. I hoped to conduct a follow-up study in Hawaii of the emigrants who had left the village I selected as a research site.

Also, in a sense I had broken with my childhood ties to the Philippines soon after graduating from college in 1968 when I joined the Peace Corps to serve as a volunteer in Malaysia. There I taught English at an elementary school on the small island of Pulau Perhentian, twelve miles off the east coast of the Malay peninsula. Thus, in returning to the Philippines, I brought with me an adult understanding of life in another insular Southeast Asian village.

For a month, in 1973, I traveled throughout the province of Ilocos Norte, looking for communities characterized by a history of emigration. A good indicator was the presence of elaborate retirement homes, fabulous monuments to success built in the 1960s and early 1970s by returned emigrants from Hawaii. Two-storied, constructed of cement blocks and expensive woods, and painted in many bright colors, the houses contrasted sharply with their humble neighbors built of hewn wood or bamboo and left unpainted. Casual conversations with villagers revealed that many thought these houses a bit garish; yet these same villagers expressed the desire to have their own and aspired to immigrate to Hawaii themselves.

There were several such retirement homes in both Bawang, located in the southern municipality of Simbaan, and Aring, a village in the northern part of the province. Aring was just a few kilometers from Banua (now serving as a camp for road workers) and was set in a lovely green and fertile valley that might have been carved from a windward Hawaiian coast. Since the 1920s, villagers had been leaving Aring for Kekaha, a plantation community on the island of Kauai.

I found Bawang's setting, unlike Aring's, unattractive. In Bawang, only irrigated rice fields were green. Unirrigated fields lay dry and cracked from lack of rain. The bamboo on the low-lying hills behind the village stood yellow and brown. Dust and smoke from cooking fires rose just a few feet above village roofs to hang in suspension, waiting endlessly for a transporting breeze.

Bawang villagers had immigrated to several different places, not just Hawaii, which would make a follow-up study more difficult. In Hawaii, most were concentrated either at Ewa Plantation on Oahu or in the Kalihi district of Honolulu. A few lived on the islands of Hawaii and Lanai. Like Berto, several plantation workers had left the Islands during the Depression to seek work as farm laborers in the San Joaquin Valley of California. As a result, there was a nucleus of emigrants in Delano. Other villagers had gone to Guam in the 1950s to work in the construction industries; some stayed and have since sent for their families. Lately, young men have taken to joining the merchant marine, and pleased parents receive postcards from such exotic ports as Havana, Amsterdam, New York, and Panama.

Despite its shortcomings, Bawang, as a research site, had attractions that Aring did not. First, in addition to planting subsistence crops of rice and corn, villagers grew garlic as a cash crop, and many traded in garlic. Cash cropping and garlic trading were relatively recent developments, dating to the late 1940s, well after emigration had commenced.

Second was the discovery that the residents of Bawang celebrated an annual fiesta. Fiestas are common at the town level in the Ilocos region but rare at the village level because of the paucity of economic resources. Peasants live in villages and a landed, professional elite resides in the towns. Clearly, Bawang villagers have acquired sufficient resources to permit them to celebrate one of their culture's most valued social institutions. This fact was more than obvious to the villagers themselves. As one entrepreneur told me, "Here we have two important products—emigrants and garlic—and that is why we are rich." When I heard these words, I immediately decided on Bawang as a research site. Bawang would permit me to study the impact of both emigration and entrepreneurship on the village's social and economic structure.

Soon after arriving in Bawang, I began to realize that the changes that had taken place in the village had not been without negative effects. Bawang had a reputation throughout the municipality of Simbaan not only for its emigrants and entrepreneurs but also for its witches. Ilocanos believe that evil spirits give witches extraordinary supernatural power. Witches use this power to make their enemies ill or cause their death. The presence of the witches implied much tension among villagers.

During my second field trip in 1975, a villager was murdered when he went to the Simbaan River at night to fish. The murder suspects were fellow villagers. This murder might not have occurred had Bawang not lost some of its most respected citizens to emigration, men and women who could have exerted controlling influence over wayward sons and siblings.

I left Bawang in 1975 with the paradoxical impression of a community experiencing both cultural renaissance and rapid disintegration. While villagers enjoyed and took pride in their fiesta, economic differentiation was increasing sharply. Only those villagers who did exceedingly well in the garlic trade or who earned dollars overseas could afford to purchase land, the culture's most valued and prestigious sign of economic well-being. Overall, fewer villagers worked themselves to the bone to maintain agricultural production while an ever increasing proportion of the labor force departed overseas. Left behind were disgruntled men and women who very much wanted to go abroad themselves but for various reasons could not.

I have tried to convey these conflicts and paradoxes in the chapters that follow by including as many stories about villagers as possible—often in their own words. These tales express themes common to leave-taking and return: loss and disorientation as well as change and resilience.

My entry into the community was eased by the hospitality of my hosts, Raphael and Estrelita Solano, and the members of their household. Raphael and Estrelita included me in many of their social and economic activities. Raphael operated a rice mill and Estrelita was a garlic trader. Both were well-liked and respected by fellow villagers and we attended many baptisms, weddings, and parties together. I enjoyed their companionship and am grateful for their generosity.

The Solanos' house was next to a dirt road that led into the village from the national highway, just a hundred yards away. The national highway linked the capital of the province, Laoag, with Manila, about four hundred kilometers to the south. From my bedroom on the second floor, I had an excellent view of the road and could watch who was entering and leaving the village. When I sat at my desk in the late afternoon writing up my field notes, villagers would occasionally look up, spot me, and wave their greetings.

In the evening I would hear only a few footsteps on the road, for most villagers went to bed early unless they were busy sorting and bundling garlic for sale the next morning. They got up early, too, often well before sunrise. Around five I would wake to the sound of the baker from Simbaan ringing a bell to attract customers for his freshly baked pan-de-sal. Would I have gotten more sleep, I often wondered, if I had told Berto that two eggs over easy would have been just fine?

Prologue:
Voices from the Past

There are many old men in Bawang who have worked in Hawaii and returned to invest their savings in land and new homes. Today, some are prosperous and others are not. Herminio saw the land that he purchased wash away during a flood when the Simbaan River overflowed its banks and cut a new course. Now he is dependent on relatives for a livelihood. What all of these men possess, however, are memories of Hawaii, memories that they shared with me:

My parents cried when I told them I wanted to go to Hawaii. They were sure that I would not return. Like a seed, they said, I would take root in the new land. Never would they see me again.

When the plantation recruiters came to our village in the 1920s and told us of the money we would make in Hawaii, we signed up —eagerly. Life in Bawang was difficult then. The rice harvests were poor. We had to hunt for edible roots in the forested hills. We had to cut down banana trees and eat the stalks.

My father mortgaged land to pay for my passage to Hawaii. This wasn't because we were poor. We had land but no cash. We didn't grow garlic in those days. I was eager to go to Hawaii because I wanted to make a dollar a day. I thought that was a lot of money.

My parents did not give me a farewell party. They couldn't afford to. No parents could afford to give their sons farewell parties then —not like today. But they did accompany me to Simbaan where I and the other recruits climbed into trucks for the long drive to Manila. There we would board the ship for Hawaii. The trip to

Manila took two days. It was September and the roads were muddy. There were so many of us in the trucks that we had to stand up for the entire journey. We felt like mules.

We were given third-class accommodations on the ship to Hawaii. We were not permitted to go up on deck. I was sick for most of the trip.

We arrived in Honolulu in the morning. We ate breakfast, then got off the ship. Authorities at the dock assigned us to the different plantations. I was assigned to Aiea. When we reached the plantation early in the afternoon, some of the laborers wanted us to work right away. But we told them we were still dizzy from the month spent at sea, and we wanted a day of rest. The men said, all right, we could rest. They took us to the plantation store to get what we needed. They told us to get some food. We could buy it on credit, they said, which meant that we could pay for it later. I got a tin of sardines, a cooking pot, and some rice. No meal is complete without rice. Later, back at the bunkhouse, the men told us that we should get up at four the next morning to get ready to go to work.

We got up at three in the morning because we were afraid that we would be late for work. We started at six. At eight we stopped work to have breakfast. At twelve we had a half-an-hour's break to eat lunch. Then we went back to work until four. Our work was very hard. I dripped with sweat. I could have wrung my clothes out they were so wet.

My brother, who had been at the plantation for a year, told me that I would cry my first day at work. He was right. The work was so hard, and my hands bled from the sharp leaves of the sugarcane. I cried and cried.

The *luna* [foreman] watched us constantly. There were thirty of us in my work group. If any of us lagged behind, he would yell, "Goddamn it! Go home and get some sleep, you weaklings!" Most of the lunas were Portuguese or Japanese. Mine was a German. He was very tall and strong. Sometimes if we worked too slowly, he would kick us. Then we would curse him in Ilocano. He couldn't understand us and this made him very angry. The first day the luna called me over. "Come here, boy," he said. He yelled to everyone to watch as he lifted me up by the chin with his large, white hands. He was crazy, but he liked me very much. Sometimes, when no one was looking, he would unbutton his trousers and make me touch his prick.

I asked my uncle what kind of work I should request. He told me to do *hopai ko* [contract work]. Instead of being paid a fixed wage, we were paid according to how much cane we loaded onto the wagons for transport to the mill. Sometimes we could make double what regular workers received. The work was difficult, but I liked it better than weeding. The lunas watched us too closely when we weeded. If they thought we weren't working hard enough, they would yell that we were "Goddamn lazy Filipinos." A luna yelled at me once. I was so angry I wanted to hit him, but I knew that if I did I would lose my job and have to leave the plantation.

The fields were burned before the cane was cut. I would return from work at the end of the day black, covered with ash. Sometimes Vicente and I would work at the mill Sunday mornings removing ash. The ash was thick and heavy. We would throw it away. Sometimes I noticed mushrooms growing in the ash. I would pick and eat them.

I visited my uncle after work. I enjoyed talking with him and his wife. And I liked watching their two small daughters play. They reminded me of my own young sisters. My uncle and his wife always invited me to have dinner with them, but I never accepted. I knew that they did not have enough food for themselves. My uncle would get angry at me and ask why I wouldn't stay to eat. I told him that I would accept his invitation the next time. But, of course, I never did. He took his family back to the Philippines after two years. They could not survive in Hawaii.

At Paia we lived in barracks with large rooms. About twenty men lived in each room. We slept on mats on the floor. Behind the barracks were large kitchens where we prepared our meals.

We had land near the barracks where we could plant gardens. Not all the men made gardens but I did. I planted eggplant, tomatoes, *saluyot* [a leafy vegetable], and papayas. There were a lot of marunggay* trees near the barracks, planted by earlier emigrants from the Ilocos. I liked to pick the leaves and cook them.

I worked at a plantation on the Big Island. Because I was older than the men I lived and worked with, I addressed them as sons. They liked me because I could cure their stomachaches. They suffered from stomachaches frequently. Sometimes the men pretended to have stomachaches because they didn't want to work. It rained often at the plantation, and the men did not like to work in the rain. But I would encourage them to go to work, to earn money to send to their families. To cure their stomachaches, I would collect a red grass and boil it, giving the men the broth to drink. This treatment worked even for men who said their penises were sore and painful. I learned of this treatment before I left the Philippines.

If I had money, I would go to the Pacific Hotel in Honolulu with some friends. A guard stood at the door of the hotel. He wouldn't let us in until I told him that I had come to visit a friend upstairs. The hotel had three stories. We rode in an elevator to the third floor. All my friends were eager to have a woman. I knocked on the door and a woman came out. She said hello and hugged me and told me that it was good that I had brought my friends along. She told me to come inside. She was a white girl. I played with her right away. My friends were surprised that I was so daring with her. They told me that I shouldn't even have the privilege of carrying her shoes, she was so beautiful. The next morning when we went to work our friends could tell that we had been to the hotel because we smelled of perfume. They teased us and told us to get away, saying we smelled like rotten fish.

Sometimes I would go to Honolulu on Saturday afternoon. I would go to the cabaret on Liliha Street and dance until eleven when it closed. The girls charged ten cents a dance. If I liked a girl I would give her a dollar so I could dance with her for a long time.

* *Moringa* oleifera, also known as horse radish trees.

There were many men in the dance hall, whites, all kinds of men. We Filipinos were the only men who treated the girls to refreshments, and they liked us for that. Because of our generosity, every time we entered the dance hall the girls would rush up to us and hug us. Going to the cabarets was the only pastime we had. Otherwise we would stay at the plantation, think of the Philippines, and become homesick.

What I enjoyed most on Sundays was cockfighting. Cockfighting was illegal, and we often got arrested. We would hold the cockfights at Mango Camp. Sometimes as many as two hundred men would bet on a fight. I made some extra money by raising roosters for Marcus Rodriguez. He ordered them from the mainland. When the roosters were big enough to fight, he would sell them for twenty dollars apiece. At the fights I had the job of boiling the dead roosters for the men to eat.

In my spare time I would go fishing—or gather snails in taro paddies. Those snails were good to eat. Hawaiians didn't like them. We would ask the Hawaiians if we could gather the snails, and they let us. Sometimes we would even catch catfish in taro patches. I made my own fishnets.

There were many different ethnic groups on the plantation—Chinese, Japanese, Portuguese, Puerto Ricans, and Hawaiians. The Portuguese, Puerto Ricans, and Hawaiians were all heavy drinkers. They would get paid one day and drink it all the next. We Filipinos were sort of like that too, but not as bad. When the Japanese and Chinese left the plantations to get easy jobs in Honolulu, we Filipinos stayed. We worked hard and became strong from the heavy labor. It is we who built Hawaii.

I sent money to my family in the Philippines three times a year. I was able to save, but saving was difficult, especially if I bought too much food at the company store. On pay day, the amount I owed the store was subtracted from my salary.

I was so anxious to save money that I would go without meat and vegetables, eating only rice.

There were many men at Ewa Plantation from Simbaan and the
neighboring municipality of Santos. Marcus Rodriguez founded the
Simbaan-Santos Association, and we all joined. This was in 1931.
We elected officers for the association. Marcus was elected chair-
man. Anytime a member of the association died, the officers collected two dollars from each member to pay for the cost of the
funeral. Members also helped each other pay for hospital expenses.

Although we were young and strong, men would die suddenly in
their sleep, without having shown any previous signs of illness.
Three of our members died in this manner. But my roommate Frederico died of pneumonia. He caught a cold when working in the
rain. He knew that he was dying, and he requested that when he
did we ship his body back to the Philippines. It was expensive to do
so. Officers asked each member of the association to contribute $5.
We were able to raise $500. This, plus the $350 Frederico had in
savings, was enough to meet the cost. We hired two bands to play
funeral music when his body was placed aboard the ship.

Members weren't asked just to contribute to funerals but also
whenever a member married or had a child baptized. Eventually, I
quit the association because I didn't think it was fair to ask us single
men to contribute to marriages and baptisms. More of us were single than married. Parents also helped pay for the cost of their children's baptismal parties by asking many people to be sponsors. The
sponsors were expected to give money to their godchildren. Whenever someone asked me to be a sponsor, I refused, saying that a fortune teller had read my palm and predicted that my first godchild
would die. This excuse worked well.

I worked at the Pahala Plantation on the Big Island. A Visayan
by the name of Pablo Manlapit came to the plantation often to
encourage us to go on strike for higher wages. To try and keep us
from going on strike, the planters brought Commissioner Ligot
from Honolulu to speak to us. He used to be the governor of Ilocos
Norte, and he was a real son-of-a-bitch. He told us that we were
lucky to be receiving a dollar a day in wages (but at Pahala we were
receiving only seventy-five cents a day!). Ligot also said we were
lucky because, unlike in the Philippines, we had spoons and forks

to eat with. Also, in the Philippines we had to go barefoot. In Hawaii we could wear shoes. Whenever he came to the plantation, he was heavily guarded, and he always left immediately after he gave his talk, never stopping to ask us why we wanted to go on strike. But we paid no attention to him, and we went on strike. The strike lasted for three months. We all ran out of money very quickly, and some of us had to leave and seek work at other plantations. The Japanese at Pahala didn't support us and continued to work— but under guard. The planters brought in new recruits from the Philippines to take our jobs. They, too, were protected by guards. Our strike was unsuccessful, and we won nothing.

I came to Ewa to join my friends, but after a couple of years, they grew tired of life on the plantations and went to California to work on farms near Stockton. I followed them. I didn't like being by myself at Ewa. I liked Stockton much better than Ewa. Even though it was the Depression, I could still find farm work. There was a lot of entertainment in Stockton. I used to go to a gambling parlor owned and operated by Chinese. I learned to shoot craps. And I often went to the whorehouses. I was so spoiled then. One whorehouse was very big. It had lots of rooms and lots of pretty white girls. Oh, I was so spoiled.

That Berto Castro led quite a life in California. He and three other men ran a pickpocketing syndicate and also robbed a couple of banks. During the Depression when he had no money he would go to a restaurant, eat a meal, then sneak out without paying for it.

By 1939 I had saved a thousand dollars and decided to try my luck in California. I was tired of working on the plantations. I worked as a farm laborer in California, Oregon, and Washington. I topped sugar beets in California and Washington and picked hops in Oregon. I didn't like the work. The pay was low. Besides, the weather was cold. In the winter I couldn't find any work. So I returned to Hawaii. There I could work every day, and the weather was always warm.

I decided to return to the Philippines when I received a letter informing me that my mother had died. I could no longer concentrate on my work. I would find myself standing there in the cane-fields at Ewa—and crying. Before I returned, I observed nine days of mourning and then held a *pamisa* [a mass and feast] in honor of my mother. I purchased two pigs which my friends butchered and cooked for the feast. A priest came to my room to pray. I invited my luna and all my friends to attend. Then, within a week, I boarded a ship for the Philippines. I returned with a thousand dollars to invest in land. I would have gone back to Hawaii, but my brother wanted to go, so I remained to farm his land—and mine. It was good to feel the mud beneath my feet as I plowed and harrowed my fields.

Enrique Comes Home

Enrique's bus was not expected to reach Bawang from Manila until ten-thirty in the evening. By seven I could see villagers beginning to gather at the roadside in anticipation of his arrival. The women chatted with each other, the children played tag; the men killed a goat, started a fire to roast it, and sent teenage boys to the nearest store to buy soft drinks, beer, and gin.

The year was 1973, and Enrique Cruz, age sixty-five, was coming home. He was returning to the village he had left forty-five years before to work on a sugar plantation in Hawaii. Since then he had never been back to Bawang—not even for a short visit. His arrival was eagerly awaited by his brothers and sisters and other members of his kindred, many of whom had been born and reached maturity during his absence.

It was the third week of May and the peak of Ilocos Norte's hot and humid dry season. The slightest wind, like a child's scuffle, stirred dust into the air. To the east, above the Cordillera Central, thunderheads had begun to form in the past few days, but none had yet moved out over the narrow coastal plains. Farmers prayed that the rains would come soon so they could plant their first crop of rice. In the meantime, they collected firewood, repaired their homes, and spent long hours along the riverbanks gathering grass for their livestock. It was a time of uneasiness and waiting. Even the social season of weddings, baptisms, and fiestas was ending, since no one was quite sure when the weather would change. Enrique's imminent return would mark the last round of celebration before villagers turned to the harrowing, plowing, and planting of their fields. Perhaps, as several of those who congregated by the roadside suggested, the culmination might be Enrique's marriage.

15

Enrique had left Bawang as a single man. As the fourth of nine children, seven of whom were male, the chances of Enrique's father providing him with a dowry at the time of his marriage were slight. In Ilocano culture a young man receives his share of the family estate in the form of a dowry at marriage. The dowry provides the economic foundation for the marriage and becomes the joint property of the husband and wife. Ideally, each child, male or female, receives an equal share of the parents' estate. But when Enrique was a young man, land was a very scarce resource. His parents did not possess enough to provide all their sons, let alone their daughters, with a dowry.

So, like many young men in his peer group and like three of his brothers, Enrique grasped the opportunity, provided by recruiters who came to his province, to work in the sugar plantations of Hawaii. This was not his only option, however. Two of Enrique's brothers migrated to frontier regions of the Philippines—one to the Cagayan Valley and the other to the southern island of Mindanao— to seek land to farm. Only Enrique's youngest brother Pedro did not leave the village. It was Pedro, of course, who cared for his parents in their old age and eventually inherited their land. Enrique's two sisters also remained in the village. Adelina married and raised a family. Esperita, like many of her peers, would remain a spinster. Because so many men had gone to Hawaii, suitable suitors were few.

The Filipino migration that had brought Enrique and three of his brothers to Hawaii was first organized by the Hawaii Sugar Planters' Association (HSPA), which represented thirty plantations on the islands of Oahu, Kauai, Maui, and Hawaii. To meet the demands of a rapidly growing sugar industry, the HSPA recruited cheap foreign labor. From the beginning in 1909, a predominant HSPA strategy was to recruit single, uneducated men in the hope of maintaining a transient, flexible labor force. As inducements, recruits were initially offered free passage to Hawaii, housing perquisites on the plantation, and after 1915, return passage to the Philippines upon completion of three-year labor contracts. The HSPA's most intense recruitment efforts occurred in the 1920s. Between 1906 and 1946 (when the recruitment ended) approximately 125,000 Filipinos went to Hawaii, most of them single men from the Ilocos region.

Not all of these men remained in Hawaii. Many, like two of Enrique's brothers, returned to the Philippines after the completion of their contracts to marry and buy land with their savings; others moved on to California to work as itinerant farm laborers. Those who stayed in Hawaii constituted the backbone of the unskilled labor force on the plantations. Few married because of the lack of Filipino women.

Unionization in 1946 would eventually make Hawaii's agricultural laborers the highest paid in the United States. At retirement, workers become eligible for monthly retirement benefits and may remain in low-rent plantation housing. They also qualify for social security benefits.

In the 1960s and 1970s many of the recruits, including Enrique, reached retirement age. Concerned with the need to provide housing for younger employees, both the plantation management and the union encouraged men to consider returning to the Philippines for retirement. If they chose to, they could receive their retirement benefits in a lump sum. An advantage to retiring in the Philippines was the favorable exchange rate of seven pesos for one dollar. In the Philippines a retiree's social security benefits made him wealthy; in Hawaii they were barely enough to make ends meet. For this reason, men like Enrique returned to their native villages, renewing ties to kinsmen and fellow villagers after what was often more than a forty-year absence.

Still single when they returned to the village, many of the men quickly married women at least thirty-five years younger and within a year or two became parents. The Philippines is fourth among foreign countries in the total number of retirees receiving social security benefits and first in the number of dependents also receiving benefits, a direct consequence of these May-December marriages.

Three-quarters of the men in Bawang sixty years of age and older have had work experience in Hawaii or California. More than half of this group returned to the village before the Second World War, shortly after completing their three-year labor contracts. Eleven did not return until they reached retirement age, and almost all of these men took young women as wives and fathered children. Because of the predominantly male migration to Hawaii, one-third of all village women sixty years of age and over have never married.

During his years in Hawaii, Enrique had not, like some emigrants, sent money to his relatives to buy land. There was no need to, for two of his brothers who had returned to the Philippines upon completion of their contracts in Hawaii had purchased land with their savings. His youngest brother had inherited land from his parents. Enrique had chosen to spend his earnings on cockfights. It was rumored among the crowd at the roadside that he had winnings amounting to thousands of dollars.

But whether Enrique was returning with part of this fortune was unimportant because he had another—the lump sum given to all returning retirees by the plantation management. Also, he would be receiving monthly social security benefits that, converted to pesos, would be more than four times the salary of a local public school teacher. Enrique's lump sum amounted to more than fifteen thousand dollars, an incredible fortune in a peasant economy.

As a young man, Enrique had left the village with only the clothing and blankets provided by the plantation recruiter, and now he was returning with a commodity that was as rare as land had been forty years before—money. While his relatives were certainly looking forward to his return, they were also a little apprehensive, for they did not know how he would choose to use his fortune. Many villagers considered the retirees to be quite selfish with their wealth.

Another repatriated retiree, Segundo Tolentino, refused to lend his nephews money they needed to join the merchant marine. (Money was needed for agents' fees and to cover the cost of airfare to Japan for embarkation.) One villager claimed this refusal revealed that Segundo did not want any of his fellow villagers to have a "progressive life." Furthermore, Segundo hired villagers to plant and harvest his rice fields instead of giving the fields to tenants to farm. His wife Mercedes even had the gall to have her maid remind villagers that debts to her could be repaid with labor at harvest time.

Segundo and Mercedes were perhaps the wealthiest couple in Bawang. Villagers estimated that their total monthly income from pensions exceeded four thousand pesos. The two were already married when Segundo went to California in 1924 to work as a farm laborer. Later, he went to Hawaii and was employed at the Makaweli Plantation on Kauai until it closed in 1948; then he moved to Oahu and worked as a janitor for the Honolulu Electric Company until his retirement in 1972. He received two pensions, one from social security, the other from the electric company.

During his sojourn overseas, he returned three times to Bawang. On his second trip in 1964 he built the house in which he and Mercedes now reside. Mercedes joined Segundo in Honolulu in 1969. The two lived in a small room in Kalihi that they rented from a fellow emigrant. Upon his retirement, Segundo built a larger and more expensive home for his only son (who died shortly thereafter) and daughter-in-law. The same year he invested seventy thousand pesos in rice land to add to his holdings. Segundo and Mercedes' hard work and Spartan life abroad assured them of comparative luxury at home.

If accused of selfishness, Segundo and Mercedes might reply that they had been quite generous to members of their immediate family, even if they did refuse large loans to other relatives. Furthermore, they hired villagers to farm their land because they had no sons to farm it for them and their grandsons were in Hawaii. Yes, Mercedes could say, she did ask her maid to request villagers to repay their debts to her with labor. She had lent many villagers money upon her return from Hawaii; few had repaid her. But she was magnanimous in valuing their labor at fifteen pesos a day rather than the customary eight.

The two might add that their spending a considerable sum the previous year to get their granddaughter elected fiesta queen (votes are purchased) assured villagers of the most magnificent fiesta ever, one that surpassed even Simbaan's in color and expense. The fiesta queen contest generated enough money to cover the cost of the three-day affair—and more. The remainder was used later to construct a shed for Bawang's only artesian well.

Nevertheless, when Mercedes was robbed of her purse (containing, she claimed, six thousand pesos in cash) at the Simbaan marketplace, villagers chuckled and said that the amount was just a fraction of her wealth, even if it did total more than her husband's monthly income from pension checks. The morning after the theft I saw Segundo and Mercedes working in their vegetable garden and stopped to chat. Mercedes asked me to inform her relatives and friends in Hawaii of her misfortune: surely, they would be sympathetic. It was the fourth time, she said, that her purse had been snatched at the marketplace.

Villagers also perceived Polycarpio Ramirez, another retiree, as
stingy. He was not one to be approached for loans, large or small.
He was the only owner of a jeep in the village, but he never offered
rides to his village mates, much to their annoyance. Furthermore,
he was a frequent complainer at public meetings, usually in regard
to the condition of the village roads or the state of the village council's finances. All the roads, he felt, should be paved with gravel, as
they got very muddy during the rainy season, so muddy, in fact,
that they became impassable, not just for his jeep—as Polycarpio
was careful to point out—but also for farmers' carabao-drawn
carts. "All we villagers need to do," Polycarpio often stated, "is borrow one of the municipal dump trucks for a week to collect gravel
from the riverbed. We could do the job ourselves, and it would cost
us nothing but labor." Polycarpio took pride in his crustiness, telling
me one afternoon, "I speak up a lot, complaining about things, and
my wife says that I shouldn't or someone will shoot me." The
thought amused him.

Polycarpio had spent most of his sojourn abroad in Delano, California, working as a farm laborer. He returned to the Philippines
when he retired in 1971. During the Depression, Polycarpio recalls,
he was paid only fifteen cents an hour—when he could find work.
"I ate only one meal a day and had only one pair of pants. But when
Roosevelt became president, things began to improve. He ordered
that people could work only eight hours a day. This meant that
many more people could get jobs. Roosevelt was one of America's
greatest presidents. It was he who gave us social security. He was
for poor people, like all Democratic presidents are." Polycarpio
acquired American citizenship during his sojourn, and when his
children were born in Bawang, he had them registered as American
citizens at the embassy in Manila.

Polycarpio visited Bawang for the first time in 1958, and he
promptly got married. He was broke at the time: in California he
had spent his earnings on cockfights and women. At his marriage
his siblings gave him his share of inheritance in land. His siblings
continued to farm the land and gave half of its annual harvest to
Polycarpio's wife, who gave birth to a son a few months before
Polycarpio returned to California. She joined him in California in
1963.

At first glance it would appear that Polycarpio's siblings suffered economically by his marriage: they gave him land that they would otherwise have kept in their possession. But in the long run, they gained, for when Polycarpio returned to Bawang permanently, he purchased rice fields with money that he and his wife had saved. Polycarpio asked his nephew, one of the hardest-working young men in Bawang, to farm the land for him. And before returning to Bawang, he sponsored the immigration of his youngest brother (and the brother's son) to California. He paid for their airfare and assisted them financially until they found jobs. From the perspective of the intervening years, it is clear that Polycarpio's marriage served to link him to his family and home in the Philippines. It is quite likely that Polycarpio's siblings encouraged him to marry during his 1958 visit, hoping that this would be the end result. Would Enrique's siblings do likewise?

As the hour grew later, more and more people gathered by the side of the road, carefully watching the sparse highway traffic. An approaching bus suddenly slowed down, and the crowd, realizing that Enrique was aboard, let out a big whoop and rushed to surround the bus as it came to a stop. The cry went up, "A Hawaiiano has arrived! A Hawaiiano has arrived!" More people rushed to the roadside. Excitement mounted; women cried and shouted; youngsters jostled each other to get the first glimpse of the Hawaiiano.

Enrique, with a head of white hair and wearing a bright red aloha shirt, stepped off the bus and was immediately engulfed by his relatives. He did not know what to make of the situation for he recognized no one. Led by his brother, he proceeded to the back of the bus to claim his luggage from the hold. Then, as the bus started up, Enrique's relatives directed him to his sister Adelina's home where he would be staying.

The next day a continuous flow of visitors came to see Enrique, many of them to collect letters he had hand carried from Hawaii. To provide snacks and a meal for the guests, Enrique's brothers and nephews, with the help of men who had reputations as skilled cooks, butchered a pig and a goat. Enrique enjoyed the attention he received from the visitors, and he willingly entertained them with stories about his life in Hawaii. On Sundays, he said, he and his friends would hold cockfights at the Waipahu Plantation. Once, he and several others went to Arizona to attend cockfights. On the way he stopped in California to visit his brother who had left

Hawaii during the Depression. Enrique's brother did not recognize him and started to cry when Enrique told him who he was. "Long time we brothers no see each other," commented Enrique to his guests. He bowed his head briefly and then shook off the unpleasant memory by changing the subject.

"I'm not going to work anymore because I have a pension." He laughed at the thought. Tapping the chair that he was sitting on, he said, "I'm going to sit here until I die. I get more than two hundred dollars a month on my pension. I came back here because I won't have to spend money on anything. I'll get a garden for my vegetables. I'll get a rice field. I'll get a house. In Hawaii I have to pay for everything: electricity, water, everything." But he mentioned that he had not decided if he would stay in the village permanently. He wanted to see first if he liked it. Already he had noticed that the air was too hot, and the wooden bed he had slept on had been hard and uncomfortable. The rice he ate for breakfast was too grainy. "Oh," he sighed to himself, "I wish I had brought some good rice with me from Hawaii."

Enrique had little intention of returning to Hawaii, but he was being careful to ensure that his relatives treated him well. The first retiree, who had returned to the village six years earlier, had been so angered by the financial demands made upon him by his kin that he and his young wife had moved to another province. Enrique, who had heard of this in Hawaii, was not about to let the lesson be lost.

Among Enrique's visitors were fellow retirees, including Segundo, Polycarpio, and Berto Castro. The latter had spent twenty years in California before being deported to the Philippines by immigration authorities for being a pimp. "Berto," said his friends, "could start across the country with a nickel in his pocket—as long as he had three girls with him."

Berto had returned to the village in the early fifties. He came back with only a small amount of savings, and his family had no land. Until he was old enough to qualify for a veteran's pension (he served briefly in the U.S. armed forces during the Second World War), he made a living by investing small amounts of money in the garlic trade. To earn prestige (which would have more easily been his if he had owned land), he invested in what he termed "public relations." When he could afford to, he gave or lent money to relatives and neighbors in need, and he often acted as the master of ceremonies at baptismal and wedding parties. He even ran for a seat on the village council and won with the highest number of votes.

Yet a gulf existed between Berto and the other retirees. He was, despite the veteran's pension, not nearly as wealthy as they were. But he did have an edge over them, and he often pointed this out: "Their public relations are very bad. These men are too tight with their money. They don't know how to be good to people. Here you are nothing if you do not have good public relations."

Although Enrique had not seen Berto since they were both young men, he knew Berto's past, and he teased him about it. "How come you leave the States, Berto? I tell you, you're no good!" Berto did not like the comment, but he accepted it good-naturedly and reached out to shake Enrique's hand.

The two could not help laughing at the changes they saw in each other. Enrique pulled off Berto's cap and chuckled at the sight of his bald head. Berto, in turn, laughed at Enrique's white hair. But he snorted at the San Miguel beer that Enrique was serving his guests. The San Miguel, a treat for Enrique, was commonplace to Berto, who demanded that he be served something imported to drink. Enrique went upstairs to his room and opened a bottle of Canadian Club whiskey. He and Berto seated themselves at the kitchen table and downed several shots. How, Enrique inquired, could Berto have a pension when he did not stay in America long enough to qualify for social security benefits? Berto explained that he qualified for veterans' benefits. He then asked Enrique for some American cigarettes. Enrique's sister Adelina overheard Berto's request and advised Enrique not to give him any. "That man already has plenty of money." Berto was annoyed at the rebuff and requested some more Canadian Club, but Enrique refused to go upstairs to get another bottle. "You come tomorrow, we drink again," he told Berto.

As he departed, Berto teasingly asked Enrique if he would be getting married. Enrique laughed and said, "I don't know. I am living with my sister, and I don't think she wants me to get married." But Enrique was wrong. Within two weeks of his arrival, his siblings had convinced him to marry. They said he would need someone to care for him in his old age.

Of course, most Ilocano men marry when they are young, and their fathers provide them with a dowry. Also, most young men marry within the village in order to keep property rights within a circle of close kinsmen and to maximize property resources, since their wives might also bring property to the marriage. But in the case of the retiree marriages, a couple of factors alter that tradition. First, a retiree establishes his own dowry by purchasing prime quality rice land, in keeping with his status as a rich man; and second, he is either too old or has no desire to farm the land himself. Thus it behooves a retiree's siblings and their children to encourage him to marry a woman from a socially unimportant family in a distant village. Geographical and social factors inhibit the wife's kindred from requesting permission to farm any of the dowry land. Therefore, the retiree's kindred have exclusive rights to it (although they share the produce with the retiree and his family).

Traditionally, if a woman is widowed before she has a child, she is obliged to return the dowry to her husband's family. As a precaution against not having children of their own, some retirees adopt children after they marry. However, all but one of the retirees in Bawang had fathered children.

Another reason a retiree and his wife start a family is the fact that natural children are a source of dollar income since they are eligible for social security benefits until the age of eighteen (twenty-two if they are college or university students). In the event of her husband's death, a young widow can support herself with her children's benefits until she reaches the age of sixty-two and qualifies for benefits herself. Polycarpio laughingly told me that if he had known he was going to live so long, he and his wife would have spaced their children every five years.

With the advice of his siblings, Enrique purchased three parcels of land, each of roughly equal value. He had no intention of farming the land himself. His brothers and nephews would do it for him. He bought no land for Adelina, his married sister, since her husband had gone to California four years earlier, nor did he buy any land for his single sister, Esperita. She would be given the job of supervising the shares and alloting the harvest, and would be awarded with a percentage of the harvest for her efforts. The three lots Enrique purchased had a total value of thirty-two thousand pesos (about $4,500).

Enrique's siblings soon informed him that they had found a girl, Perlita, to be his wife. She was the newly hired maid of Segundo and Mercedes Tolentino. Perlita was young and attractive. She had been born and raised in a small village in another municipality.

In comparison with the usual standards, the terms of the dowry settlement were quite high. They included the land Enrique had purchased, plus sixty thousand pesos. The couple would use the money to build a modern home equipped with such amenities as an electric generator, refrigerator, TV, and, for Enrique's own special comfort, a bed with a spring mattress. Enrique also promised to give a handsome gift of fifteen hundred pesos to the mother of the bride. No young man getting married in the village would have a dowry approaching this, and few ever bestowed on a mother-in-law such a generous gift.

Everyone agreed to schedule the wedding for the last week in June. It could be held no later for fear that the monsoon rains, already late in coming, would spoil the event.

The morning of the wedding Enrique and Perlita dressed early. The ceremony would be held at nine at a church in Simbaan. At eight-thirty Simbaan's vice-mayor, who had many friends in Bawang, drove the couple to the church in his jeep. Relatives and wedding sponsors rode to town aboard a bus Enrique had rented. Few people actually went to the ceremony as most were busy preparing for the subsequent celebration. At three that morning a few men had gathered at Adelina's house to slaughter a carabao and two pigs, and they were now cooking the meat dishes. Women were washing the plates and utensils to be used, preparing the vegetable dishes, and hurrying about seeing to a hundred details.

When the wedding party arrived at the church, Pedro went to fetch the priest at the rectory a block away. Everyone else stepped into the cool gloom of the church. Enrique wore a richly embroidered shirt, Perlita a flowing white dress and veil. Pedro and Adelina were dressed in new clothes tailored in Laoag. The two would be Enrique's surrogate parents for the day.

Young friends of Perlita had decorated the pews along the aisle with white crepe paper, flowers, and ribbons. Below the altar was a red cut-out heart where the bride and groom would kneel during the ceremony. At the back of the church a five-piece orchestra tuned up and, at the signal of the priest who appeared at the altar, the musicians led off with the processional, Elvis Presley's "It's Now or Never." Enrique took his young bride's arm and marched solemnly with her to the altar. At the age of sixty-five, he was getting married, scarcely six weeks after his return from Hawaii.

At ten the wedding party returned to the village where hundreds of people had gathered for the reception. A little boy shouted "They're coming! They're coming!" and the crowd jostled to get a good view of them. The two appeared hand in hand, their eyes cast down in shyness. Followed by relatives and wedding sponsors, they went into the house and upstairs to the family altar on which an offering of food had been placed and candles lit. Old women knelt behind Enrique and Perlita and began to chant a prayer, asking for the Lord's blessing. The women prayed for ten minutes, after which Enrique and Perlita rose and ritually shook hands with their sponsors. The two went back downstairs to greet their guests and take their places at the end of a long table, where, with their close relatives and sponsors, they were served the wedding meal. As soon as Enrique and Perlita were finished, they went into the house to change into informal clothes for the dance. Guests continued to be served until everybody had been fed.

Under a tent, set up near Adelina's house, chairs and benches had been arranged in a circle, the center of which served as a dance floor. A ten-piece orchestra played both traditional and modern music. Dancing had started before the wedding party returned from the church. Berto, acting as the master of ceremonies, his spirits well fortified with whiskey, enjoyed coaxing prominent guests, such as town officials, to dance. The guests chose young, unmarried girls as partners. Married women were selected only to dance the traditional *la jota* in which the male, like a proud rooster flirting with an eager hen, set a fast and intricate pace for his partner to follow.

The group was joined by Enrique and Perlita, who sat in two chairs directly in front of the orchestra. Neither took part in the dancing. Perlita had changed into an orange dress. A small, silver tiara adorned her head. Enrique wore an orange aloha shirt. If Enrique had been a young man he would have been both happy and sad, for marriage would have signified a break with the past and longtime personal relations. Often a bride and groom weep when their relatives (especially grandmothers and great-aunts) present them with their wedding gifts. Today only Perlita would be so affected.

A friend nudged Enrique in the ribs and reminded him to strap a small fish trap to his back that night. This would ensure, he said, that Enrique and Perlita would have plenty of children.

Although no one under the tent had noticed, the sky was growing dark and strong winds were beginning to blow from the south. Pedro soon realized what was about to happen and suggested the dancing stop in order to have sufficient time for the wedding sponsors to present their gifts. Godparents perform an important role in Ilocano society. It is through them that a family widens its alliance system both within the village and without, and the relationship created implies a set of exchanges. The parents of the bride and groom select the sponsors (Pedro and Adelina assumed this responsibility for Enrique), each couple choosing an equal number for a total ranging anywhere from 60 to 120 pairs. Perlita's parents and Pedro and Adelina had selected only 20 pairs. They would have chosen more except for the tradition that sponsors should always be older than the bride and groom, and this was a little difficult, considering Enrique's age. Frequently asked to be sponsors are friends, partners in trade, returned emigrants and relatives of emigrants, plus one or two Simbaan municipal officials. Pedro and Adelina had asked some municipal officials to be Enrique's sponsors as well as a few of his fellow retirees in Bawang and neighboring villages.

Adelina placed two large straw mats at the feet of Enrique and Perlita. On the mats she set three empty plates, one in front of Enrique for his sponsors' gifts, one in front of Perlita for her sponsors' gifts, and the third one in the center for tips to the orchestra. Perlita's parents and Pedro and Adelina stood behind the couple to greet the sponsors.

When all was in readiness, Berto called the sponsors in pairs to come forward to make their presentations to the accompaniment of a march played by the orchestra. Enrique and Perlita rose in each instance to shake their sponsors' hands. The municipal officials were called first and then the retirees. With their dark glasses, bright aloha shirts, and young attractive wives, the retirees added an extra dash of color to the affair. Unacquainted with local etiquette, Enrique often failed to rise in time to shake his sponsors' hands. He was reminded to do so by Pedro, who nudged him in the back.

But before all the sponsors could present their gifts, the heavens opened, and the tent began to drip, then small waterfalls gushed suddenly from every corner. Some guests rushed home, others into Adelina's house—and just in time, too, for with a shudder the tent collapsed and what had once been the dance floor was now a soggy, muddy mess. If the rains had not interrupted so rudely, friends and relatives of the couple would also have had the opportunity to present their gifts.

However, tradition was now broken and sheer gaiety took over. Enrique and Perlita went upstairs, not to appear again before their guests, and impromptu dancing commenced in the kitchen. Berto grabbed an old woman from the crowd and started to dance with her. She resisted and he grabbed another. Soon all the women were screaming in mock terror as Berto made his flirtatious advances, but they also couldn't help laughing uproariously at his antics. Any woman he grabbed broke away at the first opportunity and swatted him in the process. The mood was contagious and soon a few of the male cooks, who had had their share of *basi* (sugarcane wine) to drink, joined in the fun. The women began to flee laughing out into the rain. Gradually, as the downpour ceased, the celebrants returned home.

Enrique was married, the rains had come, and the partying season was at an end. Enrique was a landowner, and after the monsoon season he would build his retirement home. In a year he might be the father of a child, who would inherit his fortune. By encouraging him to marry, Enrique's brothers and sisters had found someone to care for him in his old age and had also helped incorporate his savings into the village economy. In the process they had increased their own wealth and prestige and helped to establish new social ties for Enrique. Now that he was married, Perlita would exercise her wifely role as guardian of his wealth and see to it that he did not squander it on cockfights and other diversions. Also, being a stranger in the village, she would not find it difficult to refuse requests for loans.

Two days after Enrique's wedding was market day in nearby Simbaan. At ten that morning a woman shouted from the national highway in a loud and urgent voice, "A Hawaiiano has arrived! A Hawaiiano has arrived!"

People who heard her thought, "Odd . . . the bus from Manila does not usually arrive at this hour." But the call was repeated. Yes, it must be so! A Hawaiiano has arrived! And men, women, and children rushed from their homes and ran to the highway taking up the call "A Hawaiiano has arrived! A Hawaiiano has arrived!"

But when they got to the highway all they found was an old spinster, Pia, standing in the center of a pile of goods that she had bought at the market. Pia needed help in carrying the provisions to her home. To get it, she used a call that she knew would attract attention. Chagrined at their gullibility but nevertheless appreciating her joke, they helped carry her belongings home.

There are many spinsters like Pia in Bawang. In comparison to wealthy retirees like Enrique, they are at the opposite end of the village social and economic spectrum. When younger, many of these women earned a living by going each year to the Cagayan Valley, a frontier region, to assist with the rice harvests. They were paid in kind for their labor. Today they constitute a labor pool drawn upon by Bawang's wealthier farmers and traders.

To secure economic and social support in their old age, many have fostered exceptionally close ties with their nieces and nephews. Most live with them, assuming roles as servants with duties of babysitting, cooking, and housekeeping. A few fortunate spinsters live in unaccustomed splendor in their brothers' retirement homes. ("My sisters," complained Innocencio Valdez, "still go to the hills to gather firewood; they won't use the kerosene stove that I bought for them.") These women have the special task of helping to supervise their brothers' land. The least fortunate spinsters live alone or share a home with another spinster; few have any land, and all must rely on friends and neighbors for gifts of rice when their own supplies are low.

In September 1975, I sat sipping beer with Enrique at the New Popular Store by the side of the national highway, near where he had stepped off the bus from Manila two years before. The proprietress of the store was Rosita Rodriguez, the only widow of a retiree living in Bawang.

Rosita had married Marcus Rodriguez. Like Enrique, he had

worked at the Ewa Plantation. Marcus had married and raised a
family in Hawaii. He was a widower when he reached retirement
age, and he decided to return to the Philippines and remarry despite
the objections of his children and grandchildren. Marcus' home
was in Santos, a neighboring municipality. Upon his return, he
asked Maria Garcia, the wife of a friend of his at Ewa, to introduce
him to someone she thought would make him a good wife. Maria
picked Rosita, forty-two years of age and still a spinster. When
Marcus proposed, Rosita said boldly that she would accept—if he
gave her ten thousand pesos. He did, plus three thousand pesos
extra!

The two were married and lived in the town of Santos in a large,
new home Marcus built with his lump-sum retirement benefits. The
house, plus a rice field he had purchased while still in Hawaii, constituted the dowry. Marcus did not buy any additional land because
he had few relatives in Santos. (Most had migrated to the Cagayan
Valley.) He did not want to have children, and he was sure that
Rosita would return to Bawang after he died. Just before his death,
he gave Rosita twenty thousand pesos as a "thank-you" for having
married him.

Rosita sold the retirement home and moved back to Bawang to
live with her brother and family. She had wanted to build a new
home in Bawang but decided instead to help her brother, Conrado
Ventura, with his transportation business. He had recently sold his
pedicab to make a down payment on a minibus and owed fifteen
thousand pesos. Rosita paid the balance and used the rest of her
money to acquire rice land as a mortgagee. Her brother did well in
his business, and he used his profits to open the highway-front
store.

Enrique and I laughed as Rosita described a marriage proposal
she had recently received, one of the many since her husband's
death. "A friend of the village captain in Sibuyas wanted to marry
me," she chuckled, "but I told him no. I said that I didn't need his or
any other man's cock to keep me happy. Marcus' had been just
fine."

As the proprietress of the New Popular Store, Rosita had settled
rather comfortably into a new life for herself. She chatted with the
store's customers to learn the latest village gossip, did sewing for
friends, and kept watch over her nieces and nephews when their

mother was busy trading garlic. Occasionally, Rosita complained about her husband's relatives in Santos, who each year gave her a smaller share of the produce from the land her husband had given her. She would not invite any of them, she said, to the pamisa she was giving in her late husband's memory two weeks hence.

Rosita withdrew to serve other customers, and Enrique, spying Innocencio Valdez stepping onto a bus for Laoag in the company of his four spinster sisters, grinned and said, "That man always used to go to the Pentecostal rallies in Aala Park [in Honolulu] and laugh at the men who presented themselves to be saved. Since he came back his sisters have talked him into joining the Crusaders' Church of Christ." Each year Innocencio traveled with his sisters (and the few other village families who were members) to the Church's head-quarters in the province of Pangasinan for a two-week retreat. There he, like other members, had built a small cottage in which to stay. On Sundays Innocencio attended services at the Crusaders' new church in Simbaan. Innocencio explained to those who would listen that he and the members of his church believed a new world order was about to be established and that the Philippines would become a major international power. President Ferdinand Marcos' declaration of martial law, for instance, was a sure sign that pointed in this direction.

As for himself, Enrique explained that he did not have much faith in religion. In 1974 his wife had given birth to her first child, a girl. The child died a week later from complications at birth, much to the couple's distress. "My daughter would have been receiving a pension now if she had lived," said Enrique. He was sorry that she had been denied the privileges due her as his dependent. "Innocencio told me that if I had prayed when my wife was giving birth my daughter would have lived. I told him that I did pray. I asked God to make my wife's baby come out. Finally, against my wife's wishes, I took her to see Dr. Manalo. It was he who made the baby come out—not God! My wife is pregnant again," continued Enrique. "Every morning I put my hand on her stomach to feel the child kick. I want my wife to give birth in a hospital this time."

In October, Enrique and his wife became the parents of a son, born by cesarian section. To make sure that Perlita did not risk her life by becoming pregnant a third time, the doctor performed a liga-tion. "Yes, I have a soldier in the family now," Enrique boasted when we met to drink beer again two weeks later. He told me that he and his wife planned to have the boy baptized in December. The rice would be harvested, the garlic planted, and many emigrants, vacationing over the holidays, would be able to join in the joyous celebration.

Faster than *Abal-Abal*

One day I was writing at my desk in the late afternoon when my host Raphael knocked on my door and asked if I would like to go to the river at dusk to catch *abal-abal*. Abal-abal are June bugs, and they appear each year at nightfall with the season's first rains. They make, Raphael pointed out, an excellent snack when roasted. Tired of writing up my notes from my morning interviews I agreed, looking forward to the adventure, if not the consumable reward.

Raphael hesitated a moment before he asked his next question: "May we use your Right Guard to help us catch the abal-abal?" I wondered how my spray deodorant could possibly be of use. Noticing the perplexity on my face, Raphael quickly supplied an answer: "Abal-abal are attracted to strong scents. We'll spray it on the branches of *kakawate** we carry. When the abal-abal come out of the ground, they'll fly to anything that possesses a strong odor. Kakawate leaves are fragrant. The Right Guard will make them even more fragrant."

My puzzled expression changed to one of amusement. "Jergen's Lotion is also good," continued Raphael.

"But I don't have any."

"I know. But Estrelita does. Maria brought her some from Hawaii."

"Then we should be able to catch plenty."

It wasn't long before Raphael called me to come downstairs—and reminded me to bring my Right Guard.

In the living room were his wife Estrelita, his mother Marcelina, and his three sons, Eduardo (age ten), Pedro (seven), and Tommy

---

**Gliricidia sepium,* also known as mother of cacao.

33

(five). His spinster aunt Doting peeked at us from behind the curtain separating the living room from the kitchen. I handed Raphael my Right Guard, and he sprayed the deodorant on the branches of the kakawate Eduardo had cut earlier. I could not discern the scent of the kakawate myself, perhaps because the early evening air was heavy with the smoke of cooking and rubbish fires. Estrelita's bottle of Jergen's was conspicuously absent. She was obviously saving it for its intended purpose.

Neighbors passing by the house on their way to the river called for us to join them. Each of us grabbed a branch of kakawate and went out the door and through the wrought-iron gate, the boys chatting happily. Marcelina and Estrelita laughed at the sight and urged us to catch plenty of abal-abal.

As we joined the growing crowd, I noticed a peculiar odor. When I asked Raphael what it was, he told me that some villagers had stripped bark from the kakawate tree on Good Friday (doing so on this particular holy day endowed the bark with supernatural power), buried it in mud, and just recently unearthed it. The mud made the bark moist, leather-like, and very strong-smelling. Villagers had cut it into strips to hang on the branches they carried.

We crossed the national highway, Rosita shouting encouragement from the New Popular Store, and went along an irrigation-ditch trail before turning to the right to take a narrow path among rice fields to a bushy, uncultivated area by the river's edge.

Just minutes after the sun set over the China Sea, a youngster spotted the first abal-abal and jumped to grab it, the surprise and concentration etched on his face breaking into a grin of accomplishment at his success. More abal-abal emerged in flight from the ground to alight on the bushes nearby and the branches of the kakawate villagers shook in their path. Villagers plucked the creatures quickly from their nesting places; only a few abal-abal escaped.

The abal-abal, contrary to Raphael's expectation, did not find my Right Guard especially attractive, preferring perhaps a rotten to a sweet odor, and I only managed to catch one. Raphael and the boys were more successful: they were quick and could catch the bugs in flight. But I was of some use. Raphael put me to work collecting abal-abal from the branches of bushes that were out of his reach.

As it grew darker, the excitement diminished. We returned to the village just as it began to rain. Neither Estrelita nor Marcelina was impressed with our catch. Doting, her eyes squinting to avoid the smoke of her cigar, marched in from the kitchen to pluck the bag of abal-abal from Eduardo's hands—not, however, before he and his brothers each reached in to grab one. While Doting roasted the abal-abal in the kitchen, Raphael helped his sons tie a piece of thread around the body and under the wings of the creature each had selected. Holding the end of the thread, the boys enjoyed watching their bugs soar in restricted flight, wings beating rapidly like a kite-tail in a whirlwind.

Raphael and I started a game of Chinese checkers, which I had introduced to the family. Marcelina watched, not letting us coax her into playing this time. Estrelita studied her notes of garlic transactions. The trading season was almost at an end. Doting soon paraded back in, carrying a pan of roasted abal-abal. "A plate, Nana," said Estrelita. "Bring in a plate." Doting shrugged her shoulders in mild annoyance but obeyed the directive. "Here, eat," encouraged Raphael, as he popped an abal-abal into his mouth and motioned to me to select one for myself. I complied and swallowed the creature without chewing. Then quickly I lit a cigarette. "Eat again," said Raphael, pleased with my effort. He had also been successful in coaxing me to eat my first dog meat, ant eggs, and snails, all exotic fare when compared to our standard diet of vegetable stew and rice. "Sure," I replied, "just as soon as I finish my cigarette." Raphael grinned at my remark. He had heard it often before. We continued our game of checkers.

If there were no restrictions on immigration to the United States, Raphael, Estrelita, and their children would leave for Hawaii faster than abal-abal fly from the ground after the first heavy rains in June. So would most villagers.

With the liberalization of the American immigration laws in 1965, Filipinos in the United States, citizens as well as permanent residents, could send for their close relatives. This process is known officially as petitioning, but villagers refer to it as "ordering," as in "My father ordered me to Hawaii" or "My son is ordering me to California." The petitioner has to prove to the immigration service that he can provide the emigrant with economic security until the

emigrant finds a job. Evidence of a healthy savings account is sufficient. But no emigrant has trouble getting a job. Almost as soon as
he steps off the plane, he applies for a social security number and
begins to look for employment with the help of relatives and
friends. Later, after he has secured employment and saved some
funds, he in turn sends for members of his family.

Between 1946, when the HSPA recruited for the last time, and
1965, only one hundred Filipinos could immigrate yearly to the
United States and its territories. This prevented married men from
sending for their families. (All married men who were part of the
1946 recruitment divorced their wives in Bawang.) Filipinos in the
United States and Hawaii could qualify for American citizenship
after July 4, 1946 (the date the Philippines was granted its indepen-
dence), if they could fulfill the literacy requirements, but few could.
As U.S. citizens, these men could have sent for their families outside the quota. After Hawaii achieved statehood in 1959, many resident aliens signed up for citizenship training classes, and Filipinos
who acquired citizenship began to send for their families.

The second phase of immigration to Hawaii did not truly com-
mence until the Immigration Act of 1965. The act eliminated the
national origins quota system and established a total of 170,000
visas with the proviso that no country could have more than
20,000 visas per year. Family reunion was a major goal of the new
immigration policy. Seventy-four percent of all visas were reserved
for applicants closely related to U.S. citizens and resident aliens.
Five preference categories were established. The first included the
parents, spouses, and unmarried sons and daughters of U.S. citizens; the second, the spouses and unmarried sons and daughters of
resident aliens; the third, skilled laborers and professionals; the
fourth, the married sons and daughters of U.S. citizens, their
spouses, and children; the fifth, the brothers and sisters of U.S. citizens, their spouses, and children. Because the first preference is
exempt from numerical ceilings, it is to an emigrant's advantage to
become a U.S. citizen if he wants to sponsor the immigration of relatives. A resident alien must wait five years before applying for nat-
uralization. A resident alien married to a U.S. citizen need wait
only three years. In 1973, the fourth and fifth preferences were
closed because of a vast backlog of applications.

Men who were about to retire and the younger 1946 recruits

initiated the second phase of immigration to Hawaii by sending for their relatives and helping to pay for the cost of their transportation. All emigrants who have left Bawang since 1965 can trace their presence in Hawaii or California to these men. This is true of Filipinos in America in general, with the exception of those who entered the country as skilled laborers or professionals. By 1970, Filipinos had become the third largest ethnic group in Hawaii, next to Caucasians and Japanese. Between 1965 and 1975, 161 men, women, and children left Bawang for overseas destinations, most often Hawaii, but also California and Guam.

A household head usually immigrates first. As soon as he can afford to, he sends for his older children who are employable, then for his wife and dependent children. Once the family is reunited, the household head sends for his mother or his mother-in-law, either of whom can care for his children while he and his wife are at work. Preparing to go abroad may take several months. Considerable paperwork is required by the American Embassy and the Philippine government. Hence the services of a travel agent come in handy. There are several in Simbaan who cater to the needs of prospective emigrants.

Once an emigrant is ready to leave the Philippines, he calls his sponsor long distance (from a phone forty kilometers away in Laoag) to tell him his flight number and arrival time. He plans his arrival for a weekend so his sponsor can meet him at the airport and have a welcome party on his behalf. At the welcome party the new arrival meets fellow emigrants from Bawang. He distributes mail that he has brought for them, and they, in turn, slip five, ten, and even twenty dollar bills into his pockets. He may receive as much as three hundred dollars. The new arrival uses this cash to cover his personal expenses (or to remit to Bawang) until he can get a job. The following Monday he goes to the nearest social security office to apply for a number. As soon as he receives it, he can begin looking for employment.

In Hawaii, most emigrants are employed on plantations, in hotels, and in the construction industry. In California, newcomers are doing what earlier emigrants did before them—living and working on the grape farms in Delano and occasionally going to Alaska to work in the canneries. The difference may be the major role labor unions play in Hawaii's economy and the rapid development of tourism in the sixties and seventies. Many of the Hawaii emigrants benefit greatly from membership in unions. A union provides an employee with job security and opportunities to learn new skills. Once in Honolulu I saw an emigrant I had met in Bawang. He was driving a large steam roller at a construction project and stopped a moment to wave at me while I waited for a streetlight to change. Just a few years before he had excelled as a farmer in Bawang, but he had no specialized, non-farming skills. He certainly did not know how to drive. His adaptability in learning new wage-earning skills is the rule among emigrants and not the exception.

Most early emigrants to Hawaii stayed at Mango Camp in housing for Ewa Plantation employees. Often those assigned to other plantations requested reassignment to Ewa in order to be with fellow villagers. Today emigrants in Hawaii reside not only in Mango Camp but also in the Kalihi district of Honolulu, twenty-seven people in two homes owned by emigrants. In Mango Camp many of the plantation homes originally intended as single family residences now house at least two families. Because real estate and rental units in Hawaii are very expensive, only emigrants with high-paying jobs can afford to purchase their own homes. Most of those who have acquired homes have purchased them in Waipahu, a community rapidly making the transition from plantation to Honolulu suburb.

In Hawaii, emigrants visit each other frequently. Social networks include not just fellow emigrants from Bawang but also from villages in Simbaan and Santos municipalities. Partying is frequent but confined to weekends. Often three hundred guests or more will attend a baptismal or wedding reception. Parties are also given for new arrivals and men who retire from their jobs. Although liquor is served at these functions, no one drinks excessively as is the case in Bawang. Parties, especially those held on Sunday evenings, come to an end by nine o'clock. No one wants to be too tired to report for work the next day.

It was difficult for early emigrants to maintain ties with their home communities. Many of the HSPA recruits were illiterate and could not engage in regular correspondence unless they had friends to write letters for them. Recruits could not visit the Philippines because the trip was long and the passage costly. However, in the second phase, begun in 1965 and still continuing, all the emigrants are literate and some are college educated. Wages in Hawaii are higher both on and off the plantations. Commercial jet transportation to the Philippines is quick and efficient, and reduced rates are available on charter flights. Consequently, the new emigrants not only correspond regularly with their relatives and friends in Bawang, but they also return to the village for vacations and family emergencies.

Vacationing emigrants have many expenses besides transportation. They are expected to shower relatives and friends with gifts, known as *sarabo,* and to sponsor a pamisa to honor the souls of relatives who have died in their absence. They must purchase at least three, if not more, pigs to feed guests. If a visit coincides with the village and town fiestas, emigrants are expected to donate handsomely to these public affairs. Finally, on the eve of departure, they are expected to invite friends and relatives for drinks and snacks. In addition to these obligations, vacationing emigrants often rent buses to take their relatives to the city of Baguio for a weekend. Located high in the Cordillera Central, Baguio has long been a summer retreat for the wealthy. All of these cash outlays, of course, add up. One young man in Hawaii told me that he would not consider returning to Bawang for vacation until he had saved at least three thousand dollars. His airplane ticket would cost about $650; he would spend the rest of his money on entertainment.

Emigrants also keep in touch with their relatives through the mails. The village postmaster distributes numerous airmail letters from abroad daily. A record of all incoming mail is kept at the post office in Simbaan, and recipients must sign for their letters. This helps protect the mail carrier from accusations of theft. Money is sent through the mails, but most of it is carried to Bawang by vacationing emigrants (or by an anthropologist returning for his second field trip: an emigrant in Kalihi gave me twelve hundred dollars to take to his wife).

As villagers see relatives, neighbors, and friends go overseas, many express disappointment at not being able to go abroad themselves, particularly those who have petitioned for visas but are listed in the fourth and fifth preferences. Many villagers have acquired extra land to farm when relatives emigrated, and some live in new or renovated homes financed with remittances. But most see this as small compensation.

My host Raphael says that he would eat his own shit if he could only join his father Donato in Hawaii. Donato is easily Bawang's wealthiest emigrant. The owner of a small farm and three houses in Waianae as well as a home in Kalihi, Donato works as a stevedore on the Honolulu docks.

He went to Hawaii in 1946 as part of the last HSPA recruitment, but worked on a plantation only a few months before finding more lucrative employment as a stevedore. He made his first real estate investment in Hawaii in 1955 when he purchased the farm and houses in Waianae, a rural section of Oahu noted for its high percentage of native Hawaiians. Donato rented the house to non-Filipinos and, after sinking a well, began a truck farm, selling produce on his days off to his many Filipino friends.

In the early 1960s he purchased a large house in Kalihi, a residential district in Honolulu that is predominantly Filipino. His brother, also a stevedore, owned a house in the valley just a short distance away. As the second phase of immigration to Hawaii commenced in earnest, both men, because of the resources they controlled and their personal wealth and generosity, became patrons to the new emigrants. The two subdivided their houses into several small apartments and rooms, which they rented at reasonable rates to the newcomers. Close relatives came to stay. Most others used the residences as stepping-stones, places to live cheaply until they found employment and could afford to rent or purchase a home or apartment of their own. Those who found high-paying jobs in the construction industry made this transition most quickly.

Donato also invested in real estate in Bawang. Returning to the village in the 1960s, he built a modern, two-story home for his family. He also purchased rice land and a rice mill (set up in a shed behind the house) for Raphael to operate. Raphael was slight and did not take to working in the rice fields. He gave his land to tenants to farm and spent his time operating the mill. Raphael's wife Estrelita meanwhile speculated in the garlic trade, and when he wasn't busy at the mill, he assisted her. Just a year before I first arrived in the village, Donato sent Raphael money to purchase a second rice mill. The first one was dismantled and shipped to the Cagayan Valley, where it was operated by Estrelita's pioneer cousins at a charge of fifty cavans of *palay* (unhulled rice) per year. Marcelina and Doting had the responsibility of traveling to Cagayan twice a year to collect the rent.

Donato had ordered Raphael and Estrelita to Hawaii but the fourth preference closed before their papers were processed. Both were convinced that the preference would not open again, and, if it did, that Donato would do nothing on their behalf. This was due to the fact that Donato had divorced Marcelina and remarried. His second wife happened to be Estrelita's cousin, and the woman had just borne Donato a son. Donato had sent word to Raphael and Estrelita via returning emigrants that, despite their pleas, he would no longer offer them economic assistance. He had, he emphasized, more than adequately provided for the two already. They derived income from the land he had purchased as well as the two rice mills, and they lived in the handsome house he had built during his vacation in the 1960s. Certainly this was enough: his income now had to be directed to his new family in Hawaii. Estrelita never hesitated to wonder—somewhat cynically—how much her cousin had to do with this decision: were Donato's remittances now being sent to her relatives? Despite Donato's decision, Raphael and Estrelita always sought out vacationing or returning emigrants to see if Donato had sent them any money. I was with Raphael once when he visited a vacationing emigrant, one who happened to rent an apartment from Donato. Yes, Donato had indeed sent them a letter. Inside were three crisp five-dollar bills, one for each of his grandsons but none for Raphael or Estrelita. Raphael was chagrined and embarrassed at what he perceived to be his father's miserliness.

Divorce is illegal in the Philippines, but it is easily obtainable in Hawaii. Like the other four women in Bawang divorced by their emigrant husbands, Marcelina had no reasonable means of contesting the divorce other than ignoring the court orders sent to her, hoping that by doing so the judge would not grant the divorce. She was wrong, as Donato's remarriage proved. Neither Marcelina nor the other three women can remarry. As far as Philippine law is concerned, they are still married.

On his visit to the Philippines in the 1960s, Donato had heard rumors that Marcelina, during his sojourn abroad, had been unfaithful. Donato had become incensed, particularly when he was told that the man she had slept with was his cousin. "I told her she should not have opened her trunk for another man," Donato told me when I visited him in Honolulu. "Because the man was my cousin," he continued, "I could not forgive her."

Marcelina denied committing adultery, but Donato chose not to believe her. Some villagers say that Donato was justified in his accusation; others say he was not. For the rest of his visit he would not speak to Marcelina, and he remained unmoved when she approached him one afternoon while he was resting to plead her case. Marcelina left his side weeping, and she wept for hours afterward.

Marcelina is the obvious victim of a double standard. Prior to his remarriage, Donato had two common-law wives in Hawaii, and he fathered a child by each. Marcelina knows quite well what she has lost. She is constantly reminded by visiting emigrants that her former husband is the wealthiest emigrant in Hawaii. "Oh," a returned emigrant sighed to me one day, "if Donato had ordered Marcelina to Hawaii she would be sitting pretty. We would all be envious of her."

There was no chance of Donato sending for her now, but Marcelina did have a better chance of going abroad than Raphael. Her daughter Perla (Marcelina and Donato had only two children) had married an emigrant, and in 1973 Perla and her family were residing in Torrance, California, where she worked in a factory. Perla had two young sons, and she needed someone to care for them while she and her husband were at work. She hinted in letters she wrote to Marcelina, Raphael, and Estrelita that she might consider ordering Marcelina to California on a first-preference visa if she was willing to come. Marcelina did express interest, and this distressed Raphael and Estrelita, for it was Marcelina who cared for their children and managed the household when they were busy buying and selling garlic. Also, if the fourth preference opened and, miraculously, Donato ordered them to Hawaii, there would be no one left behind to care for their sons. The whole family could not afford to immigrate to Hawaii at once. If Marcelina went to California, who would mother her children? Estrelita wondered.

Marcelina might have suggested Doting if she hadn't known better. A nervous, jumpy woman, Doting was not altogether reliable. Raphael and Estrelita's three sons frequently annoyed her. She had little authority over them, and the boys were often disrespectful. When the annoyance grew too great, Doting would wrap her belongings in a blanket that she balanced on top of her head and march out of the house, muttering that she had had enough of the three little devils and doubted if she would ever return. Doting's destination was the home of another of her sisters-in-law whose husband was also in Hawaii. Her abrupt departure was always the source of some amusement to those she left behind who knew that she would be back in a few weeks—as soon as her temper cooled or her sister-in-law's own children began to annoy her.

Quite suddenly in 1972 Raphael and Estrelita thought they might have the opportunity to go to Hawaii. Donato's (and Doting's) brother, the owner of the house in Kalihi, died unexpectedly of a heart attack. His widow sent a telegram to the village announcing the death, saying she would pay the round-trip airfare for some of his relatives to come to Hawaii to attend the funeral. Raphael, Estrelita, and Doting were among those to whom the invitation was extended. Immediately they and eight others packed their bags and left as a group for Manila. Raphael included in his luggage a new scythe that he hoped to use working on his father's Waianae farm.

The group's first stop in Manila was the American Embassy to obtain temporary visitors' visas. All knew that embassy officials had granted villagers visas to go to Hawaii during family emergencies and that the officials would undoubtedly do so again. They were correct, but the officials granted only two visas—one to Doting and the other to her sister. All the others had applications on file to emigrate, and the officials, believing that they would be unwilling to return to the Philippines after the funeral, refused to grant them visas. Raphael and Estrelita, as well as the others who were denied visas, were very disappointed. They were so disappointed, said Doting, that neither would go to the airport to bid her farewell.

After the initial stress of the funeral, Doting greatly enjoyed her stay in Hawaii. Her relatives and friends were generous to her when she arrived—each of them gave her ten or twenty dollars for spending money. She bought a new dress and decided to save the rest of it for her return. The money was her nest egg. As a propertyless spinster, she had no security but the good will of her relatives.

Doting stayed in her deceased brother's home and assumed the responsibility of getting up each morning at three o'clock to prepare breakfast and a box lunch for the many household members who worked, giving her sister-in-law who normally performed this task a rest.

Donato wanted Doting to remain in Hawaii permanently and even consulted a lawyer about the matter. Doting, Donato told the lawyer, should be permitted to stay in Hawaii because she had no property to support herself in Bawang, and he was willing to support her in Hawaii. The lawyer replied that the only way Doting could remain in Hawaii was to marry. Doting shuddered at the prospect. She certainly was not about to do that, not at her age. Besides, as she explained to Donato, as days and then weeks passed, she began to miss her life and friends in Bawang. She looked forward to returning home. So she selected a date and a reservation was made for her return flight. Before her departure, she used some of her money to buy an aloha shirt for Raphael and perfume and lotions for Estrelita and Marcelina. Upon her arrival in Bawang, she gave Raphael fifty dollars, and she lent Estrelita two hundred dollars to invest in the garlic trade (Doting arrived back just at the start of the season). Sometime later, Doting left Raphael and Estrelita's house one day in anger after her request for repayment of the sum from Estrelita had been refused. Estrelita told Doting that she had more than repaid the loan—in room and board. Weeks later, Doting quietly returned to the house and resumed her role as kitchen maid. Raphael and Estrelita, meanwhile, continued to dream of going to Hawaii.

The second evening after I moved into the Solano home in March 1973, Raphael and Estrelita received a telegram from their cousin Leon Bumanglag (the son of Marcelina's sister) saying he would be arriving the next day on a bus from Manila. Leon had been in the merchant marine for a year working on a German freighter. He didn't mention the reason for his return in his telegram, but he did say that he had many problems. I learned later that his ship, needing repairs, had been placed in dry dock in Hamburg for five months. Neither Leon nor his friend, also from Bawang, could find work on another freighter so the shipping company gave them plane tickets for Manila, with no promise of future employment. The two did not want to return to the Philippines because they predicted that it would be next to impossible to leave again: martial law had been recently imposed by the government. It had been difficult enough for them to leave the Philippines during normal times. Leon, his friend, and eight other young men from Bawang had each paid an agent three thousand pesos to find them employment with the merchant marine and to arrange their papers to go abroad. The fee included airfare to Japan where they would board their respective ships. The young men found no jobs awaiting them in Yokohama. They had to seek employment on their own. Leon and his friend were lucky: they found jobs on a German freighter after just a week. The others eventually found work on Greek-registered freighters and tankers. Aboard ship Leon worked as a dishwasher.

Leon sent a telegram to the Solanos rather than to his own parents, who lived in a neighboring village, because before going overseas he had been a member of their household. He had helped Raphael operate his rice mill and assisted Raphael and Estrelita with their garlic trading. Leon was a hard worker and the opposite of his father, a lazy man who liked to gamble. His mother would come by the Solano house to complain about her husband to Marcelina. He had, she would say, just lost again heavily and mortgaged a rice field to pay his debts. How would she feed her family (one other son) if her husband continued in this way? Marcelina listened sympathetically, but not Estrelita. She was annoyed with the woman. Why couldn't Leon's mother assume her responsibilities as a wife? It was up to her, after all, to manage the family's finances and make sure there was enough food on the table. If doing this meant keeping her husband from gambling, then she should keep him from gambling. It was that simple. To Estrelita, there was no such thing as a bad husband—only a weak wife. Leon's mother was weak.

Leon arrived in Bawang early in the morning, having taken a night bus from Manila (which had to stop beside the road for four hours from midnight to 4 A.M. to observe the curfew). Everyone from the western end of the village ran down to the roadside to greet him, and his friends helped him carry his bags to the house. Twenty-three years of age, Leon was a friendly-looking, stocky young man. He greeted the Solanos with a great deal of warmth, and they were delighted to see him again. He brought balls for the two older boys and a music box for Tommy, the youngest. He gave Raphael a pair of binoculars. For himself he had bought a handsome tape recorder and radio. Leon tuned it to a popular radio station as Raphael went next door to purchase some beer to serve Leon's friends. Leon had already taken a bottle of scotch from one of his bags and poured rounds for his friends in glasses provided by Marcelina and Doting.

Within minutes, Leon's father arrived. He shook hands with Leon quietly upon greeting, and Leon gave him his gift—a wristwatch. He examined it quickly before slipping it into his pocket. Perhaps he did not want his creditors to see it in his possession. Leon's mother then rushed in and began to wail and cry when she saw her son, exclaiming, "Oh, my son! My son!" She kissed him and ran her fingers through his hair, exuberant that Leon had come home.

Greetings complete, Leon's parents hurried back to their village to prepare a feast for Leon and his friends, which the Solanos and I later attended. About a hundred people were present. A pig was butchered for the occasion, and the beer, gin, and sugarcane wine flowed plentifully. Although Leon spent most of his time with his friends, he did spend a few minutes visiting with the vice-mayor of Simbaan, who had heard there was a party, as well as with Berto Castro and some of his fellow village counselors from Bawang. Leon spoke briefly of his overseas experiences, mentioning that Panama reminded him of the Philippines and that he had enjoyed visiting Disneyland in the company of Raphael's sister and family. Aware that Leon would not have returned to Bawang so soon if his ship had not gone into dry dock, no one asked him what his future plans were.

In the middle of the afternoon we went back to Bawang. Raphael and his friends promptly butchered and roasted a dog, a favorite snack, so that when Leon returned from his parents' home, there would be something to eat. Around five o'clock Leon and his friends arrived. For the next three hours, they joked and sang songs until the friends gradually began to drift home, some quite drunk, others in an exhausted stupor. The day's partying had taken its toll.

Leon, however, had been quite careful about the amount of alcohol he was consuming, and he was ready to sit down to a special chicken dinner prepared by Marcelina and Doting. As we were eating, Doting asked Leon what job he had performed on ship. Estrelita gulped—surely Doting already knew the answer. He replied that he had washed dishes. "Oh," she said, shrugging, with a trace of disgust, "that's woman's work." Leon did not comment.

Estrelita changed the subject. Laughingly, she asked Leon if he had any plans to go to Hawaii. She knew, as did everyone else at the table except myself, that Leon's longtime sweetheart, Maria Lopez, would be vacationing in the village with her parents soon. Maria and her family had gone to Hawaii five years before. There she had graduated from high school and was now employed as a clerk in a mortgage company. Leon replied that he considered himself on vacation from the merchant marine and that he hoped to join up again. He would still be aboard ship, he said angrily, if it weren't for that "shitty, fucking, goddamn captain" who made the decision to put the ship into dry dock.

Leon's insistence on rejoining the merchant marine was likely a face-saving device in the event that Maria, to whom he placed a long-distance call from Laoag three days later, refused his marriage proposal. Maria didn't, and her father, Jose Lopez, with whom Leon also spoke, gave his approval. The two would be married in Bawang during the Lopezes' vacation.

Leon discovered that the time between his phone call and the arrival of Maria and her family passed with agonizing slowness. The night before the Lopezes were to arrive by bus from Manila, Leon slept by the roadside, just to be sure he was there to greet them.

When the Lopezes arrived, Estrelita and Raphael were, at least at first, somewhat in awe of Maria. During her five years in Hawaii, Maria had changed in ways her parents had not. Certainly her parents were a little plumper and healthier in appearance. (Ricardo, a friend of Jose's, told me that Jose looked younger: "He must have an easy job.") However, the manner in which they perceived their home and culture was essentially the same. This was not true of Maria. In adapting to Hawaii's culture she was becoming alienated from her own, perhaps because she had spent some of her formative years in Hawaii and had been exposed much more directly to its multiethnic environment than her parents. Her own awareness of this was apparent in the frequent comparisons she drew to her life in Hawaii. For example, when we ate a meal at the Lopez home during our first visit, Maria expressed amusement at my use of a spoon, which is customary in the Philippines. "This is the way I eat now," she laughed, pointing to her fork. Nor did Maria bother to conform to local fashion. Rather than wear a dress, she had on shorts and a tank top. This caused no embarrass-

ment to anyone present: they had expected Maria to change, and
she met their expectations.

Three days after the Lopezes arrived, Leon's parents and close
relatives, Marcelina included, visited the family to discuss the wedding plans: where and when the wedding would be held, and what
would constitute the dowry. Because Leon wanted to join Maria in
Hawaii as soon as possible, it was decided the two would be married in a civil ceremony within a week. Then the marriage could be
registered at the American Embassy and the petition papers filed.
Maria was an American citizen, which simplified matters. If there
were no bureaucratic foul-ups, Leon would be able to join her
within six months. A second wedding would be held at the Philippine Independent Church in Simbaan three weeks later, with a
reception to follow at the Lopez house.

Leon and Maria commenced their married life after the civil
wedding. Until her parents' departure, the couple spent their nights
at the Lopez home, with Leon's parents, or with the Solanos, moving from one household to the next every three days or so.

The day before the church wedding, I accompanied Marcelina to
Leon's house for the presentation of the dowry. Here members of
Maria's kindred met to formally receive the dowry from Leon's kindred. Relatives of all ages were present, but it was older members
of the kindreds who performed the crucial roles, not the parents of
the bride or groom. Neither Leon nor Maria was present.

We gathered on the second floor of the house. On a large straw
mat had been placed several sealed bottles of vintage basi (white
paper flags signifying agreement attached), two plates of glutinous
rice, and one empty plate. Two women, representing each kindred,
sat ramrod straight at opposite ends of the mat like a buyer and
seller at the marketplace about to engage in heated bargaining. The
bargaining, of course, had already taken place, the terms of the
dowry negotiated. What followed then was entertaining and sym-
bolic. An elder of Leon's kindred read from a list the parcels of land
that would constitute the dowry. The location of each lot and its
history of ownership were described in detail. (Marcelina had told
me earlier that Leon's father, in addition to giving Leon land to constitute the dowry, would also have to mortgage land to pay for the
cost of the wedding reception. This was of great concern to him
because he had already mortgaged some fields to pay for Leon's

entrance into the merchant marine—and to pay off his gambling debts—none of which had yet been redeemed. However, investing in Leon's marriage was also investing in his own future: his son could one day order him and his wife to Hawaii.) The elder was occasionally interrupted in his reading by questions about the property. When he finished, he handed the list to the woman representing Leon's kindred. She tossed it haphazardly into the empty plate at the opposite end of the mat—as if her action were of no major consequence. As a result, the woman representing Maria's kindred mocked its value: "Surely," she said, "Maria's hand in marriage is worth more than this?"

"And where," she continued, "is the money that constitutes part of the dowry settlement?" Leon's representative, all the while extolling the exceptional value of the land given in dowry, untied a handkerchief and withdrew some peso bills that she tossed into the plate, one after the other. The money symbolized Leon's family's willingness to pay for the reception and other wedding expenses, such as Maria's wedding and reception dresses.

As she slowly stacked the bills into a neat pile on the plate, Maria's representative complained further, "Is this really all you're going to give us?" she asked. Like a customer who simply had to have the item at hand, no matter what the cost, Leon's representative tossed more bills onto the plate, sighing as she destroyed the neat pile. Would this merchant's demands never cease?

But Maria's representative was still not satisfied. "Come now," she coaxed, "won't you just give me fifty centavos more?" With a grand gesture, Leon's representative tossed a polished silver peso onto the plate.

Maria's representative was satisfied at last; the property and cash settlement were complete. Next, Leon's representative presented the boxes containing Maria's wedding and reception dresses. Maria's representative opened each box and inspected the dresses carefully. She signaled her approval by reaching for one of the bottles of basi, opening it, and pouring a drink for herself and Leon's representative. More bottles were quickly opened and general merrymaking commenced. I had never before been present at an occasion when women drank, but here they freely did so. As I drank from a glass passed to me, Marcelina told me to snack on some of the glutinous rice. Doing so, she said, would keep me from getting drunk. The merriment did not last long, however, as members of Leon's kindred had to return home and prepare for the wedding-eve dance that night.

Less than three weeks after the couple's wedding and reception, Maria and her parents returned to Hawaii, Leon to follow as soon as he received his visa. The night before their departure, Raphael, Estrelita, and I joined the Lopezes, their friends, and relatives who had gathered at their home for an informal farewell party. We took a shortcut through rice fields, resting once in a grove of trees where we wiped our brows with cool water that Raphael drew from a well. The night air was warm, and we were perspiring from our short walk. Estrelita asked Raphael if he had his *anib,* an amulet carried for protection from witches. Yes, he did. Did I have mine? she asked, always the concerned hostess. I nodded affirmatively. Estrelita was unsure who might be at the party and did not want us to take chances. Earlier in the year two garlic traders had fallen ill and died. Villagers suspected that a witch had made them sick. Witches are believed to receive their malicious power from evil spirits. By touching their victims and offering them food, witches can cause illness and even death.

When we arrived at the Lopez home, we found most visitors crowded into the single upstairs room where Maria and her mother Chelito were finishing their packing. Chelito reminded Maria not to take all her wedding presents with her for Leon could bring some when he came. One reason Chelito made this request was that visitors had asked her to take packages of candy, dried fish, and dried shrimp to relatives in Hawaii, and she had affably agreed to do so. Raphael strung a scale from the central beam to weigh the luggage. That morning he had used the scale to weigh garlic he and Estrelita had purchased in a neighboring municipality. The weight of the luggage exceeded the Lopezes' allowance by many kilos. Maria began to unpack more of her wedding presents to leave for Leon. Meanwhile, Chelito relaxed briefly by sipping a cup of coffee and sitting down to count all the letters friends had asked her to take to their relatives: the total was well over a hundred.

Outside in the courtyard youngsters were dancing to the hard beat of rock music from a battery-operated record player. Two old women imitated the dancers in exaggerated fashion, and their antics evoked much laughter. Those inside began to peer out the windows to see what was happening. The next dance was a slow drag, and the young couples held each other at a discreet distance. The two old women, however, mischievously lunged at each other like two hot lovers and swirled about the yard. Likewise, Leon's father grabbed a young man by the buttocks and danced with him, grinding the young man's hips into his own. The fun lasted less than a minute, and when everyone had stopped laughing, the two old women began to sing. The mood of the evening changed instantly. "How sad," they intoned, "are we to see the Lopezes leave. Let us hope that they will remember us. Let us hope that they will one day return." The women danced to their song in short and graceful steps.

Abruptly, Maria's father Jose, who had been sitting with friends in the doorway of his home, fell ill. He complained of weakness and dizziness. Alarmed, his friends carried him upstairs to lie on a wooden bed. Chelito instructed a nephew to run quickly and fetch an *ambulario,* a healer. Like a witch, an ambulario has special ties to the spirit world, but he is given the power to heal, not to harm. Jose's symptoms indicated that he was suffering from *an-annong,* a debility caused by a ghost's caress. The ghost, most likely that of a recently deceased relative, was saddened at the thought of Jose's departure and had reached out to touch him. Clothes were placed on Jose's chest to draw the weakness from his body. When the healer arrived, he massaged Jose's temples and shook leaves of the kakawate tree over him. He confirmed that Jose was suffering from an-annong but said he would be better in the morning. He was.

At seven, the Lopezes walked to the national highway with their friends and relatives to wait for the bus that would take them to Manila. The trip was part of their charter package. Leon had already secured permission from the bus company to ride with the Lopezes to Manila. He and Maria would check on the progress of his visa application at the American Embassy.

A friend of the Lopezes told me at the roadside that Jose had become ill the night before because he had been upset at the thought of leaving. "When we were at the house this morning, we avoided looking at each other so that we wouldn't begin to cry. It is hard to be apart so long."

When the bus arrived, the Lopezes could no longer maintain their graceful composure. They cried as they embraced their relatives and friends, who cried in turn. Leon, eager to bring the scene to an end, urged the Lopezes onto the bus as fast as he could. When it pulled slowly away from the curb, Leon's mother saw her son's face in the window. She screamed for him in anguish, as if he had just died. "Oh, my son!" she cried out, "Oh, my son!" Soon there was no trace of the bus except a cloud of dust.

As the crowd at the roadside began to disperse, Raphael teased Leon's mother, who was still weeping. "Why did you cry out so for Leon? He isn't leaving for Hawaii yet. He's only going to Manila!" She acknowledged her mistake by grinning as she heard those about her begin to laugh.

Five Pesos a Dance

From south to north along the dirt road that leads into Bawang are three homes, all built within fifty yards of each other. The first belongs to Filomena Corpuz and her husband. Filomena is Bawang's most successful garlic entrepreneur. She earns a small fortune each season buying and selling garlic. She has invested her profits in rice fields and also in a passenger bus that runs the route between Simbaan and Laoag. In 1975 she decided it was time to rebuild her house. The new version would be as big as a Hawaii retiree's—but not painted in the same garish colors. Filomena's problem was that her lot really wasn't large enough to suit her purpose. But she had a simple solution. She would appropriate land from her neighbors to the north, the Guevaras.

The Guevara house was built of bamboo and thatch. The Guevaras were also garlic traders, but not very successful, for they owed Filomena and village traders a great deal of money, more than they could ever afford to repay. This was Filomena's wedge, and she used it to her advantage. She would, she said, consider the Guevaras' debt to her repaid if they gave her a strip of land, four meters wide, along the northern border of her property. The Guevaras could do no less than agree, even though it meant dismantling their kitchen to clear the land. Filomena then proceeded with her plans to enlarge her house while the Guevaras pondered where to rebuild their kitchen.

A few weeks later, the Guevaras sought, like Filomena, to extend their house lot by appropriating land from their neighbors to the north, Teodoro Ruiz, his wife, and his elderly mother. Teodoro's father had immigrated to Hawaii in 1946. On one of his trips back to Bawang, he had built a house for his wife and son. He later

53

divorced his wife in the Philippines and remarried. He has since completely severed his ties to his Bawang family, much to their distress. Recently, with the assistance of a Simbaan lawyer, Teodoro's mother applied for the social security benefits rightfully due her. The back benefits she was entitled to meant she would receive a large lump-sum payment, expected to arrive any day. Everyone in the village, including the Guevaras, knew this.

The Guevaras' rationale for seeking to extend their property was the fact that they owned a small piece of land on the opposite side of Teodoro's property, and they claimed that a part of the Ruiz house—the kitchen—extended onto this property. The Guevaras wanted to trade one-and-a-half meters of this property for an equivalent strip on the southern side of Teodoro's property next to their house. This arrangement would give the Guevaras room to rebuild their own kitchen.

Teodoro was not happy with the Guevaras' proposal: he insisted that his kitchen did not extend onto their property. After an angry mid-morning exchange, both parties agreed to ask Ernesto Valdez, onetime village counselor, to help them settle the matter. Ernesto measured the boundaries of both properties with a tape measure and concluded that Teodoro's kitchen did indeed extend onto the Guevara property. At this point, the Guevaras made a new proposal: they would sell their strip of land to Teodoro for fifteen hundred pesos. Teodoro said he wasn't interested in a purchase but he would agree to a trade.

Teodoro's mother, who had remained indoors without comment, suddenly stepped outside. She was outraged at her son. He was weak-willed, she said; he shouldn't have caved in to the Guevaras' demand. Stung, Teodoro yelled at his mother to be quiet and not interfere. Instead, she shouted that she would never trade any land to the Guevaras. If they didn't like a portion of her kitchen being on their property, she would remove it. She ran back into the house, entered the kitchen, and started kicking at its walls, as if to dismantle it.

What, onlookers asked her, was she doing? She replied that she was tearing the house apart because this side of it belonged to the Guevaras. The onlookers laughed and urged her to desist—there was, they assured her, no immediate need to tear her kitchen apart. Besides, she would hurt herself kicking against the kitchen's hard wooden walls. It was not made of bamboo and thatch as the Guevaras' had been. His mother's performance, however, did not convince Teodoro to change his mind.

The Guevaras next suggested that a cement block wall be built between the two properties. Teodoro liked this idea and said he would be willing to share the expense. But surely, the Guevaras commented, Teodoro could afford to pay for the wall himself— since he had a father in Hawaii, while they had no relatives overseas. The Guevaras might have added that Teodoro's mother would soon be receiving a pension. Teodoro firmly said no: he would build the wall only if the Guevaras shared the expense.

Both emigration and entrepreneurship have greatly accentuated social and economic differences within Bawang. Investment in land by current and returned emigrants has so inflated its value that only villagers who have access to dollars or who have done exceptionally well in the garlic trade can afford to purchase it. Villagers recognize this emerging differentiation and comment both ruefully and humorously that they can classify themselves into the same grades by which they classify garlic: "big," "middle," and "small."

Emigration has not only led to changes in social and economic relations among villagers; it has also changed the relationship between villager and Simbaan townsman. When migration to Hawaii began in the 1920s, many village farmers were tenants of Simbaan landlords. Some villagers had their own land to farm as well; others did not. The competition for tenancy rights was intense, and, as a consequence, Simbaan landlords manipulated the traditional patron-client tie to their advantage, extracting more from the exchange than was their due.

Typically, the relationship between upper-class landlord and lower-class tenant is characterized by two types of exchange. The first is economic: the tenant pays a percentage of the crop for the right to farm a piece of land. The second is social: the tenant and his wife perform errands and provide services for their landlord. In turn, the landlord acts as a sponsor at their children's baptisms and marriages and helps the tenant secure legal advice and settle tax problems if the need arises. Ideally, the goods and services exchanged between landlord and tenant are seen as gifts that accompany an economic relationship.

But former Bawang tenants of Simbaan landlords recall that in the 1920s and 1930s they were expected to provide their landlords with services but could not expect to receive anything in return, even in times of scarcity. "Our landlords would not extend rice to us on credit. If we had no rice, we had to look for edible roots on the hillsides or cut down banana trees to eat the stalks," remembers one tenant. Almost certainly for this reason, tenants rarely asked Simbaan landlords to be sponsors at baptisms and marriages.

The opportunity to immigrate to Hawaii gave Bawang farmers the chance to save money to purchase land and build new homes upon their return home. Those who returned to Bawang before the Second World War bought irrigated rice land from their former landlords in Simbaan. Landlords in the Ilocos region had begun to take advantage of two new opportunities that presented themselves during the American colonial period: entry into the professions and politics. They began to sell off their holdings to raise funds to pay for the education of their children or to sponsor their own political campaigns. Ironically, the men who had the resources to buy the land were the sons of peasant farmers in the villages.

Today, retirees returning to Bawang purchase land for their dowries from fellow villagers (or farmers in neighboring villages) who find themselves in debt or are anxious to pay for their own overseas emigration. This is true also of current emigrants who choose to invest in land, although few actually do, preferring instead to sponsor the emigration of their relatives or to send remittances to dependents. While retirees have tenants farming their land, they have not assumed the traditional role of an upper-class landlord who acts as patron to his client tenant. Three reasons may account for this. First, a retiree's tenants are all close relatives (younger brothers, nephews) who have played an important part in easing the retiree's transition to village life. They have helped him select a spouse and found land for him to purchase as dowry. Second, unlike the upper-class landlords, no retirees own more than a hectare or two of land. The high price for irrigated rice land militates against their acquiring more and therefore having to seek anyone but close relatives as tenants. Third, again in contrast to the upper-class landlords, the retirees do not have important extra-village social and economic ties. They know few lawyers or politicians who could, if the need arose, provide services for them or their relatives. Retirees are thus very much patrons without power. In fact, members of the upper-class in Simbaan—both professionals and landlords—do not accord the retirees equal status, despite their wealth, because the retirees are of peasant origin and are uneducated. When retirees are not present, municipal officials often ridicule them at public gatherings.

As emigrants continue to leave Bawang for Hawaii and other overseas destinations, more land becomes available for those who remain behind to farm. This is beginning to change the traditional share arrangements. Frequently, all the male members of a sibling set have emigrated. Their wives, who remain at least temporarily in the village, generally allocate rights to farm their land among their own brothers and nephews—precisely what the siblings of a retiree attempt to avoid when they encourage him to marry a woman from a distant village. Since these women receive regular remittances from their husbands, they are not dependent solely on the productivity of the land. Hence, in some cases, their "tenants" keep a larger percentage of the harvest for themselves. The traditional division is two-thirds to the tenant and one-third to the landlord for garlic, and fifty-fifty for rice. But these women are satisfied with receiving only a fourth of the garlic harvest and a third of the rice harvest.

Current patterns of emigration appear to be creating a labor shortage for some village families, which may result in pressure to further liberalize share arrangements in favor of the tenant. In recent years several landless young men and their wives have moved to Bawang from other villages in the Ilocos region and from Pura, Tarlac, in Central Luzon, which used to be a destination for Bawang migrants. These men farm land belonging to emigrants and even live in homes that emigrants have vacated. I myself know of two cases in which young single men, both from other villages, have been incorporated into Bawang households—that of a retiree and of an emigrant—in order to perform household and farming chores. Furthermore, Bawang has a reputation within the municipality of Simbaan for the degree to which its women engage in agricultural tasks normally performed by men.

For villagers who cannot seek wage work abroad, garlic trading is the principal means of engaging in the cash economy. Some villagers make up deficits in rice production through trade. Those few with greater capital assets earn profits that permit investment in land as well as other entrepreneurial endeavors.

When I first visited Bawang in 1973, the garlic crop had just been harvested so traders were at the peak of their activity. Men and women cleaned and bundled garlic from early in the morning until late at night to prepare it for sale. Garlic was everywhere— loaded onto oxcarts, jitneys, and buses that bumped along village roads, stacked from floor to ceiling on front porches as well as in living rooms and kitchens, and spread on canvas in the noonday sun to dry. A few kilograms of the best garlic were even hidden away in upstairs rooms like silver pesos to be sold when their value increased.

Farmers from Santa Catalina, a cash-crop producing area in Ilocos Sur, introduced garlic to Bawang farmers in the 1940s by renting land from them to plant garlic. Within two years Bawang farmers stopped renting their fields to the Santa Catalina farmers and began to sell garlic to them instead. Many of the Santa Catalina farmers began to assume full-time roles as traders. They transport- ed the garlic to the city of Vigan and shipped it from there to mar- kets in the province of Pangasinan and also to Manila.

In the 1950s the Philippine government prohibited the importa- tion of garlic from Taiwan in order to protect local growers. This action increased the selling price of garlic and undoubtedly stimu- lated not only more garlic production but also more small-scale trading. By 1960 in Ilocos Norte the municipality of Simbaan was second only to Dingras in garlic production. Most Bawang farmers began to trade in garlic and became regular suppliers of Santa Cata- lina middlemen, who in turn supplied large-scale wholesalers in Manila. The fact that Bawang is next to the national highway and only forty minutes by bus from Santa Catalina helped promote trading.

After garlic is harvested in January, it changes hands many times in a complex network of trade. Each trader occupies a particular niche in the movement of garlic from field to consumer. The amount of capital a trader wishes to invest and the commercial and social ties he or she has to other traders usually determine the niche a trader occupies. For instance, in Bawang there are three types of traders. First, there are wholesalers who have considerable capital to invest and who have established fictive kinship ties to middlemen from Santa Catalina by asking them to be the godparents or wedding sponsors of their children. As a consequence, Santa Catalina middlemen advance capital to them for investment. Such ties generate strong sanctions for meeting obligations. In turn, much of this capital has been advanced to Santa Catalina middlemen by Chinese merchants in Manila. If market conditions permit, these wholesalers engage in trade throughout the year. There are four such wholesalers in Bawang, three women and one man.

Second, there exist what might be called "companies," composed of two to ten people who join together to invest small amounts of capital in trade (usually generated by selling produce or livestock). Companies form at the beginning of the season and continue—with only one or two exceptions—until the first rains in June when farmers must turn their attention to preparing their fields for the rice crop. Not all members have the same amount of capital to invest and some do not have any. Nevertheless, they all share their profits—and losses—equally. This may appear unusual, but company members are often closely related or are neighbors. Also, and perhaps of greater importance, while capital is a critical asset, successful trade requires other skills and resources that may be of equal value. One person may be especially adept at bundling garlic; another may have critical ties to suppliers, and so forth.

Each company is headed by a captain, usually male (except when all the members are women), who makes most of the commercial decisions and who provides most of the capital for investment. The captain is not, however, entrusted with the capital of the other members. All go together to buy garlic. Each member may spend his or her capital on a particular purchase, or all may pool their capital for one major purchase. When the capital of each member has been spent, the company takes the garlic to the village where members sort, clean, and bundle it for sale to one of the four village wholesalers.

Except for those companies bound by kin ties, membership usually changes from year to year and may even change during the course of one season. Some companies are formed exclusively of women, only a few exclusively of men. At the peak of the garlic season there are about sixteen to twenty companies in operation.

The third type of trader might be termed the Bulacan small traders. This group usually consists of single women who purchase garlic (frequently on credit) either from their parents, the wholesalers, or the companies to sell in Bulacan Province near Manila. Bulacan is ten hours by bus from Bawang and there are numerous markets in the area. The women sell garlic in bunches of a hundred to vendors, or they retail it themselves bulb by bulb or clove by clove. Turnover is slow, so the women have joined together to rent a house. About ten women engage in this activity.

Although there is a small amount of trade in garlic at the local marketplace in Simbaan, very little garlic is channeled through such marketplace networks. Traders go directly to the farmers, who sell their crops at their own discretion. A farmer may choose to sell garlic in the fields before it is harvested, immediately after it is harvested, or not until it is thoroughly dried. Garlic does not spoil once dried, nor is it subject to insect infestation. A farmer may store it for as long as a year. Thus the decision as to when to sell may rest on a number of other considerations. For example, a farmer who does not have to sell at harvest to meet cash needs may choose to wait for an increase in price. Most farmers in Simbaan municipality hold onto their garlic until several months after harvest, hoping for a price jump. A good supply of garlic is stored in many a farmer's home, awaiting discovery and purchase by traders.

Little emigrant wealth is channeled into the garlic trade. Retirees and their wives prefer to keep their vast capital resources in Laoag banks. Frequently, however, the wives of emigrants are approached for short-term loans or enrolled as investors themselves. When opportunities for high and rapid profit exist, members of garlic companies often turn to such women for capital to make larger purchases of garlic. The women are incorporated as temporary members of the company for a single transaction. They are given an equal share of the profits but are not expected to contribute their labor.

These women are interested both in helping fellow villagers by loaning money for trade and in making money themselves. While the remittances they receive from their husbands give them a measure of security, by no means are they as wealthy as the wives of retirees. Some may even face the threat of divorce, in which case remittances would stop altogether. A couple of women have actually become seasonal full-time traders in their own right.

The rewards of entrepreneurship are not as great as those associated with overseas emigration. Except for the wholesalers, most garlic traders only make enough profit to meet living expenses. The few wholesalers have done well for themselves. They have used their profits to invest in land, build new homes, pay for the education of their children, and invest in the transportation business. Unlike retirees, the wholesalers are key members of the local economy. They purchase garlic regularly from farmers and small-scale traders to sell to Santa Catalina middlemen, and they loan substantial sums of money at high interest rates to villagers eager to support their sons' entry into the merchant marine. In addition, they run for local political office. Unlike retirees, wholesalers are very much patrons with power.

Both emigration and entrepreneurship have accentuated economic differences among villagers as well as altered the relationship between villagers and upper-class townsmen. Bawang's fiesta illustrates these two changes. The fiesta gives wealthy villagers an opportunity to earn social prestige by redistributing a portion of their resources to the community at large, and it also gives villagers an opportunity—by staging a more costly and elaborate fiesta than Simbaan townsmen—to thumb their noses at their former landlords.

To celebrate his daughter's just having been elected fiesta queen, Conrado Ventura took off his tennis shoes and tied one to each end of a five-foot-long bamboo pole. He lifted the pole to his shoulders and paraded about in a circle, much to the amusement of his fellow villagers. Then he tied a piece of paper to the pole and set it afire, evoking more laughter. Spotting a dirty piece of mat lying on the ground, Conrado picked it up and placed it on his head. He had just spent thousands of pesos to get his daughter elected fiesta queen. Now he was playing the fool, relaxing and rejoicing in his victory.

It was four in the morning and the few villagers who had slept the night would soon be rising. The rest would stumble home and try to get some sleep before the heat of the day set in. The last canvassing for fiesta queen had just taken place and Julie Ventura, fourteen years old, had been elected with seven thousand pesos in votes. Votes are purchased, and the money is used to pay fiesta expenses. In all, seventeen thousand pesos had been raised in the balloting.

The fiesta is produced by the Bawang Progressive Club, and most villagers, except the poorest, are members. The club was founded in 1966, the year of the first fiesta. Members are divided into eight groups, and each group assumes responsibility for nominating a candidate for fiesta queen. Every member takes a turn sponsoring a candidate. Members without a daughter of the appropriate age (between twelve and sixteen) can "borrow" one from someone in their group. Thus all members have the opportunity to get a daughter—real or fictive—elected queen.

A group raises money for its candidate by assessing members an agreed upon sum and by selling refreshments at each of the two canvassings. Most of the votes for a winning candidate, however, are purchased by the candidate's family and friends. Not surprisingly, all winners have come from the village's wealthiest emigrant or trading families. Conrado, however, was neither an emigrant nor a garlic trader. He owned a passenger bus that ran the route between Simbaan and Laoag. Just a year before he had borrowed money to purchase the bus from his sister Rosita, the widow of retiree Marcus Rodriguez. Conrado had done very well in his business. Now, by getting his daughter elected fiesta queen, he gained considerable social prestige.

The canvassing took place in a field south of Innocencio Valdez's house. Here the fiesta celebrations would also be held. Club officers had prepared for the event by setting up a kerosene-powered electric generator for lighting and borrowing a blackboard from the local school to keep track of the vote tallies. Each candidate was provided a table and chairs, all arranged in a large semicircle.

By nine o'clock, hundreds of villagers had gathered to "vote" for their favorite candidates and to enjoy the evening's festivities, which included dancing. Just as things were getting underway, Sergeant Bulding of the Philippine Constabulary command in Simbaan drove up in his jeep and announced to club officers that the canvassing would have to cease promptly at eleven-thirty so everyone could be home by midnight, the curfew hour. Club officers were annoyed, but were careful not to express their annoyance to Bulding. Rather, they poured him two glasses of his favorite scotch, and, as he drove back to town, handed him the unfinished bottle. They knew that once he started drinking, it was difficult for him to stop, and they decided to proceed as planned.

Berto Castro acted as master of ceremonies. He instructed villagers to seal their contributions to their favorite candidates in envelopes and write the candidate's name—as well as their own, if they wished—on the envelope. Then they should place the envelopes in the large box he set on a stool in front of the blackboard. He warned that envelopes with no candidate's name on them would be considered contributions to the club, and he ruled that any dollars donated to a candidate would be converted to pesos at an exchange rate of seven to one. Envelopes could be placed in the box at any time.

The first special event of the evening was a fund-raising dance. A string band from Simbaan had been hired especially for the occasion. Men selected their partners from among the candidates. A single dance cost each man five pesos. The candidates were inexperienced dancers, and they were often out of step with their partners. But the men didn't seem to mind. They winked knowingly at their friends who were chuckling on the sidelines.

Before the first of three vote countings, Berto auctioned off food prepared by each of the eight groups: fish, fried chicken, and pork. He established an opening bid for each item based on a shrewd assessment of who in the group could afford it. Group members bid on their own items. If a visiting emigrant belonged to the group, the opening bid was high.

The first of three countings proceeded quickly as most villagers were saving their votes for the final balloting to add as much suspense to the event as they could. As each envelope was opened and its contents counted, Berto announced the amount, the name of the donor, and the recipient. Club treasurer Manuel Valdez kept a running tabulation on the blackboard of each candidate's total.

There was more dancing, a second counting, and finally the prospect of the third and final counting. At this point, Julie Ventura led her closest rival Madelyn Pascua by only ₱190. Looking at his watch and noticing that it was almost three in the morning, Berto loudly urged voters to cast their ballots, emphasizing that the balloting would cease in one minute. He continued making this announcement for thirty minutes. Realizing that Berto was unwilling to bring the balloting to an end, club officer Hilario Tolentino assumed control. He looked pointedly at his wristwatch and announced in a booming voice that the balloting would cease in exactly five minutes. There would be no extension. No one doubted Hilario's authoritative word. This was it.

Tony Cabanban, club president, was a member of the group sponsoring Nena Estacio, one of the leading contenders. He strutted about the semicircle and proclaimed that Nena would surely win. Wasn't her grandmother, he asked, Amparo Estacio, one of the village's most successful garlic traders? As Tony boasted, Hilario began the final countdown, and the crowd began to shout in excitement. Madelyn Pascua's mother rushed forward and deposited several envelopes into the box just before Hilario pounced on it. Conrado, father of Julie, also rushed forward but Hilario declared the balloting at an end and waved him away. Conrado didn't stop and Madelyn Pascua's father jumped up and blocked his path. For an instant the wild cheering ceased. Would Conrado draw a knife and stab Madelyn's father? Did the envelopes he held in his hand contain the pesos needed to assure his daughter's victory? No one knew the answers to these questions except Conrado, and he suddenly burst into laughter. His envelopes were empty, he said; he had already deposited more than enough money to guarantee his daughter's victory.

Everyone relaxed, but just for a moment. Tony Cabanban angrily walked up to the ballot box and claimed that he had not heard Hilario's announcement bringing the balloting to an end. He insisted that balloting be continued for another two minutes at least. Villagers shouted no: it was clear to them that Tony simply wanted Nena to win. Two minutes would give Nena's grandmother the opportunity to deposit more money on her behalf. They had all heard Hilario. Why hadn't Tony? Nena's father Tante brought the matter to a quick end by stating he didn't think the balloting should be reopened. His mother looked relieved: she could save her money to invest in garlic. The last counting commenced, Tony sulking on the sidelines.

Soon it became clear that Julie Ventura, daughter of Conrado, had won handily with a total of nearly seven thousand pesos, four thousand more than her nearest rival Madelyn Pascua. Part of the total seventeen thousand pesos raised would be rebated to each candidate to help pay for her fiesta gown. The remaining funds would be used to cover fiesta expenses. Any surplus would go toward a special project, decided upon by club members, to benefit all village residents.

Villagers raised more money in their contest than Simbaan townsmen did in theirs, much to the chagrin of municipal officials, especially the mayor. The mayor was worried that Bawang would someday evolve into the center of a new sub-municipality, cut from Simbaan's existing boundaries, an idea that appealed to village and municipal officials not friendly to the mayor. Already Bawang is the largest village in the municipality and its residents obviously the wealthiest. A proposal to make Bawang the center of a new sub-municipality might be well met by provincial authorities.

In contrast to the Bawang fiesta, a moveable feast, the Simbaan fiesta is always held April 7 on St. John the Baptist's Day. St. John the Baptist is the town's patron saint. Villages in the municipality are expected to participate in the Simbaan fiesta by marching in the parade, and village officials are expected to be present at the coronation of the queen. This year, 1975, Bawang villagers did not participate in the event for two reasons: they were busy preparing for their own fiesta, planned for two weeks later, and Diony Bautista, village captain, failed to tell them when the parade and coronation were scheduled. The mayor was not pleased.

He ordered municipal police to summon village officials to his office, and there he lambasted them. Their absence at the parade and coronation had been a source of great embarrassment to him, he said, and he was considering cancelling Bawang's permit to hold a fiesta. He would announce his decision in Bawang the next morning: Diony Bautista was to make sure villagers were present to hear what he had to say.

In the morning the mayor's anger had still not abated, and he sharply criticized villagers for not marching in the parade. He regarded their failure to do so as a personal insult, and he suspected that villagers didn't march in the parade because of an incident that had occurred at Bawang's first canvassing for fiesta queen. Simbaan's vice-mayor, no personal favorite of the mayor but well-liked by Diony Bautista and his friends, had become rip-roaring drunk as he often did at village social functions. For some reason—no one in the village knows why—the vice-mayor yelled that municipal officials, including himself, would not give Bawang permission to hold a fiesta. The vice-mayor was wrong, the mayor said. No municipal official ever had any such intention. Had villagers ignored the Simbaan fiesta because they believed the vice-mayor's pronouncement?

The mayor didn't get an answer to his question, but villagers told me later that the mayor was incorrect. They never paid much attention to what the vice-mayor said even when he was sober. The reason they hadn't participated in the fiesta was that Diony Bautista never requested them to. Diony was an irresponsible village captain, they said, and they were more annoyed with him than with the mayor.

The mayor continued his tirade, now attacking the vice-mayor. The vice-mayor, he said, got drunk too often, spent too much time in Bawang with his friends, and, as a result, greatly neglected his official duties. Recently he had heard that the vice-mayor and some of his Bawang friends had brought a prostitute from Laoag and set her up in business for two days and nights in an abandoned shed by the Simbaan River. Villagers, the mayor emphasized, should have brought this illicit activity to his attention. He invited villagers to tell him who the vice-mayor's cronies were. No one responded, but they could have told him that one was Diony Bautista. A man, continued the mayor, should be satisfied with one woman, his wife, and not seek out prostitutes for pleasure.

The mayor then changed the topic and told villagers to take a greater interest in municipal affairs and not be so self-centered. He singled out Arturo Magbaleta, current village counselor and former captain, for having lost interest in village affairs because of his impending departure for Guam to join his son and daughter-in-law.

But despite all the faults he found with the village and its officials, the mayor announced that he had decided to let Bawang go ahead and have a fiesta. After all, villagers had helped elect him, and he was grateful for that. He hoped, however, that relations between village and town would be more harmonious in the future.

After quickly drinking a cup of coffee prepared by Estefania Burgos, village counselor, the mayor drove off in his jeep. Philippine Constabulary Sergeant Bulding, who had accompanied the mayor to Bawang, remained behind. He leaned over to me and said that the mayor had asked him to come along because he was afraid that someone would try to injure him. Noticing suddenly that villagers were dispersing, the sergeant quickly jumped to his feet.

Since he had made villagers observe the curfew at their last canvassing, he announced, he was giving them permission to break it during the fiesta. Villagers applauded his decision, laughing to themselves as they did so.

The fiesta turned out to be a great success. What especially
pleased Bawang Progressive Club officials was the fact that the
fiesta ended handsomely in the black. As a result, they had seven
thousand pesos at their disposal. Meeting privately, they decided to
use three thousand for a project and deposit four thousand in a savings account to be used to assist club members during emergencies.
Officers called a meeting of club members to decide on a project to
support. At the meeting spirits were high, for no one had anticipat-
ed the fiesta would meet with such financial success. After much
discussion everyone agreed that a section of village road should be
paved, a stretch that got very muddy during the rainy season, making it almost impassable even for carabao-drawn carts. With three
thousand pesos, officers calculated that they could purchase 150
bags of cement and 10 truckloads of sand and gravel from a company in Laoag. Club officers agreed to go to Laoag the next day to
place their order. Work on the project would begin the following
Wednesday, labor to be volunteered by members of the club. Those
who didn't show up would risk losing their club benefits, and no
substitutes under the age of fifteen would be accepted.

Before the meeting broke up, Tony Cabanban, club president,
made an unexpected announcement. He said that the mayor had
recently called him into his office and suggested that the Bawang
Progressive Club make a "voluntary" contribution of fifteen hundred pesos to the new Simbaan sports center (not much more than a
cemented basketball court and plaza surrounded by a low wall with
lampposts for lighting). The amount, the mayor had told Tony,
would be sufficient to pay for one lamp post. The club's donation
would be commemorated on a plaque at the base of the post.

"There goes our road," a villager complained. "We won't have
enough money to pave even a small section of it now." Village counselor Estefania Burgos suggested facetiously that the club pay for
the lamppost by installment. Then she urged that since the contribution was optional, the club only contribute five hundred pesos, if
that. Knowing that it was impossible to hold out against the
mayor's wishes, Tony Cabanban emphasized that he was in favor of

making the full donation. If the club didn't make a donation, he stressed, Bawang residents would be ashamed to show their face in Simbaan. Besides, the donation would be a source of pride for the village. Furthermore, he knew that the neighboring village of Sibuyas was making a donation to the sports center. Bawang could do no less.

Ricardo Valdez urged Tony to find out how much Sibuyas was contributing. He explained that if Sibuyas was giving only one hundred pesos, Bawang could give two hundred and thus keep most of its fiesta earnings for the road project while upstaging Sibuyas at the same time. Tony made one final suggestion: that the club proceed with its plans for the road project and make the donation to the sports center. This would be possible if club members agreed to use some of the club's emergency funds for the donation. They did, and spirits picked up as once again they began to talk enthusiastically about the road project.

The Bawang Progressive Club is modeled on the older but still functional *sociedad,* of which there are two in Bawang. The original sociedad was founded before the Second World War by returned emigrants from Hawaii. It in turn is modeled on the regional association that evolved among Simbaan and Santos emigrants at Ewa Plantation. The Simbaan-Santos Association was (and is) essentially a funeral association, men contributing equal sums of money to help cover the costs of member funerals. Realistically, funerals were about the only life-cycle event the HSPA recruits could anticipate. Few could hope to marry because of the demographic imbalance in the Filipino population and the considerable racial prejudice that prevented them from marrying into other ethnic groups.

When Esteban Magno returned to Bawang in 1931 after four years of work in Hawaii, he and two friends, one also a returned emigrant, decided to form a sociedad ostensibly to help villagers meet the expenses associated with marriages and funerals. Actually, the sociedad was a means of elaborating these affairs. Esteban and his friends solicited one-peso contributions from each villager who joined and used the money to purchase plates and cups, instruments for a string band, and tables. These items became the corporate property of the sociedad, to be used without charge by members (nonmembers could rent them for a fee). As members of the sociedad, villagers assisted each other in sponsoring feasts by contributing firewood for cooking and loaning blankets for shade tents. They also contributed a fixed sum to the family of any member who died to help meet the costs of the funeral. Prior to the founding of the sociedad, villagers attending a wedding or funeral feast would make donations of cash or rice to the host, who listed the donations in a notebook for future reciprocation. The founding fathers of the sociedad, later becoming its officers, assumed this task on behalf of their members. They also made sure that members met their responsibility to the sociedad by overseeing work groups and collecting funeral contributions.

To encourage villagers to join the sociedad, Esteban and his friends decided to sponsor a fiesta, the first ever for the village before 1966. Three girls were candidates for fiesta queen. The winner was the daughter of an emigrant who sent remittances to assure her election. The money was used to pay for a feast. A second—and at that time, final—fiesta was held the next year. By this time most families in the western section of the village were members. Two years later villagers in the eastern section formed their own sociedad. Esteban reports that it was not long before the institution spread to other villages in the municipality. In recent years each sociedad has solicited contributions by mail from members residing overseas to buy new cups, plates, and musical instruments.

Like the Simbaan-Santos Association, Bawang's two sociedades are institutions associated today with an older generation of men, those who had the opportunity to immigrate to Hawaii as HSPA recruits. In 1966 a younger generation of men, several of whom were sons of returned emigrants, founded the Bawang Progressive Club. Membership was open to all male residents of the village, thus crossing membership lines drawn by the two sociedades. Like the sociedades, the club is a funeral association and a mutual aid society, offering financial assistance to members, and to some nonmembers, who suffer catastrophe. But club members, unlike those of the sociedades, do not assist each other in giving feasts associated with the life cycle. Rather, the club takes the responsibility of sponsoring and organizing a community-wide celebration: the yearly fiesta that has become a village institution in the past ten years.

No comparable organization has evolved among the current

group of emigrants in Hawaii and California, many of whom save their money to return to the village during fiesta time. In effect, the fiesta encourages emigrants to maintain ties with their home community by providing them with a means to achieve social recognition as wealthy individuals, either by directly sponsoring a candidate for fiesta queen or by making generous monetary contributions to help pay for prizes and entertainment.

Both the sociedades and the fiesta are important institutions reflecting the character of social life in Bawang. In the first phase of immigration to Hawaii, the sociedades enhanced lateral ties among villagers and, in doing so, strengthened social solidarity. Thus the sociedad institutionalized an earlier, informal pattern of reciprocity. Because membership was broad-based, social functions such as marriage and baptism doubtless became more elaborate. Membership in the Bawang Progressive Club is also broad-based but, while all members have an equal opportunity of getting their daughters elected fiesta queen, only a few actually have the resources to do so. The family, then, whose daughter is elected queen demonstrates its wealth and the strength of its social ties. In the eight fiestas that have been held, four in the sixties and four in the seventies, one queen was the daughter of a garlic entrepreneur, four were the daughters of emigrants, two were the daughters of men farming considerable land for their emigrant relatives, and in 1975 the queen was the daughter of Conrado Ventura, who received financial backing for his transportation business from his sister, the widow of a retiree. Thus, while the fiesta reflects the reciprocal ties that bind villagers together, it is also very much a reflection of the unequal access villagers have to prized economic resources.

Reservations for the Next World

In 1974 Wilfredo and Pura Castro spent three weeks visiting Bawang. They lived in Guam but returned to the village each dry season. The day before their departure, the Castros gave a party for their relatives and friends. Many attended, not only from Bawang but also from the neighboring village of Sibuyas. All enjoyed feasting on the two pigs the Castros had purchased for the event. The party itself was uneventful, with two exceptions. The village captain Diony Bautista got into an altercation with Maximo Espiritu. Diony accused Maximo of stealing some of his garlic, and Maximo hit Diony over the head with a beer bottle. Friends quickly separated the two before the fight got worse.

Also, Pura Castro noted that Virginia Solano of Sibuyas followed her about and occasionally tried to touch her. Such behavior was unusual, and it disturbed and even frightened Pura. What, she wondered, was Virginia up to? Although Virginia was the grandmother of one of her daughters-in-law, Pura did not know the woman well. Further, she had heard rumors during her visit to Bawang that Virginia was a witch. Ilocanos believe that witches are able to cause illness and even death, a power bestowed upon them by malicious supernatural beings. Witches must use this power or be killed themselves by the spirits.

Nevertheless, Pura dismissed the incident until she fell ill in Manila before boarding her flight. In Guam, her illness did not abate. She constantly felt dizzy and feverish. Concerned, Wilfredo took her to one doctor after another, none of whom could diagnose or cure her. As a result, Pura convinced herself that Virginia had made her ill. She pleaded with Wilfredo to take her back to the Philippines. She wanted to consult an ambulario. Unlike doctors trained in Western medicine, ambularios are believed to have the power—bestowed upon them by powerful spirits—to cure illness. Wilfredo complied.

Three weeks after leaving Manila the Castros were back again, and they immediately sought out an ambulario in neighboring Quezon City. In no time at all the ambulario confirmed Pura's suspicions. Yes, her illness had been caused by a witch, and the only way she could recover was to gain possession of something belonging to the witch, preferably an article of clothing. Wilfredo and Pura would have to return to Bawang.

Once there, Pura persuaded her daughter-in-law to go to Virginia's house in Sibuyas and take one of her dresses. This was an easy task for the daughter-in-law because as Virginia's granddaughter her presence in Virginia's house was not suspect. When the dress was in her possession, Pura pressed it to her chest and immediately felt better. Her dizziness and feeling of weakness vanished, evidence that Virginia was truly a witch.

Word of this, of course, reached Virginia, as it did most everyone in Bawang and Sibuyas, all of whom had been wondering why the Castros had returned so soon after their visit. Virginia trembled with fear and rage. She knew she was not a witch, but how could she make anyone believe her? Villagers also blamed her for Justino Gomez's recent death. Justino was from the neighboring municipality of Santos. There he had become very ill, and his symptoms were bizarre. He would run a high fever. When it lapsed, either one of his arms or legs would be paralyzed and would remain so until the fever started in again. This cycle continued for weeks. Weary of his relatives in Santos, and they perhaps of him, he went to Sibuyas to live temporarily with his sister Potenciana, a neighbor of Virginia. Hearing of his illness, Virginia visited Justino and massaged his paralyzed limb. She told him not to worry about being sick: he was young and strong; he could look forward to a long life as a successful farmer.

Potenciana was absent when Virginia visited. She was angry when she learned of the visit because she suspected Virginia was a witch and thought Virginia might have caused Justino's illness during an earlier visit to Sibuyas. Virginia learned of Potenciana's suspicions and became incensed. Was this the way, she cried, for Potenciana to reciprocate her kindness to her brother? Virginia marched to Potenciana's house, drew a knife, and stabbed Potenciana in the hip. Potenciana's cousin Domingo grabbed Virginia, preventing her from inflicting more injury. Domingo dragged Virginia back to her house while relatives rushed the wounded Potenciana, bleeding and in shock, to the hospital in Simbaan. The relatives then informed the municipal police of the incident, and the police quickly went to Sibuyas and arrested Virginia. They detained her in the municipal jail for a month and, upon release, ordered Virginia to compensate Potenciana monetarily.

Not long after this incident, Domingo was killed when he fell from a tree while chopping firewood. His brothers believed that Virginia had caused his death out of spite for having prevented her from killing Potenciana. To bring her malevolence to an end, the brothers decided to kill Virginia. Hearing that they were searching for her, she hid in a granary. They did not find her.

It was at this point that Wilfredo and Pura returned to Bawang seeking a cure for Pura's illness. Distressed that they, too, suspected her of being a witch, Virginia decided to kill herself in Pura's presence. She believed this would prove to others that she was not a witch: she was free to take her life at will and not dependent on evil spirits for her continued existence.

Virginia took up a long, sharp bolo that she used to cut firewood in the hills behind Sibuyas and walked along a trail to Bawang, screaming her intentions along the way. She attracted a crowd that followed after her, a safe distance from the reach of her bolo.

In Bawang, Virginia first stopped at the Solano home and begged Marcelina to accompany her to the Castros. Fearful, Marcelina refused. Virginia cried out that she could no longer live with the knowledge that villagers believed her to be a witch and that she was going to kill herself in Pura's presence. But without her noticing, Filomen Gorospe, a municipal policeman from Bawang, approached Virginia from behind and skillfully disarmed her. She was furious at him for taking her bolo and insisted nevertheless on proceeding to the Castros'—until the elderly and respected Arturo Magbaleta persuaded her to return home.

A few days later, Suzante, one of Domingo's sons, found Virginia alone, sweeping her yard. He approached her silently and stabbed her three times in the neck, breast, and hip. He fled, and Virginia fell to her neatly swept yard and began to bleed to death. Her children found her and took her to the hospital in Simbaan, where she told municipal police that Suzante had attacked her. She died three days later.

Virginia's children took her body back to Sibuyas where they washed and dressed it before proceeding immediately to Simbaan for a funeral service and burial at the cemetery on the outskirts of town. No one except Virginia's children attended the funeral. Whatever their feelings about their mother's death, Virginia's children kept silent: they did not want her reputation as a witch to be transferred to one of themselves.

Marcelina told me this harrowing story when I asked her one day if witches in Bawang could make emigrants in Hawaii ill. Only, she replied, if they happened to be in the village visiting. I asked her if she believed Virginia had been a witch, and she replied in the affirmative. Witches were dangerous and powerful, she reminded me, and I should keep my distance from two other suspected witches—Amparo Estacio and Diosdado Tolentino.

The Solanos had warned me about Amparo and Diosdado when I first arrived in Bawang in 1973. Estrelita had Raphael prepare me an anib, an amulet to protect me from evil spirits and witches. She realized that I would be meeting and talking with many villagers, including Amparo and Diosdado. Despite the fact that the anib should protect me, I was to avoid Amparo and Diosdado if possible and not let them touch me ("If they touch you, touch them back—but don't let them notice"). I must not eat any food or drink they might offer me. The anib consisted of a few grains of salt, the heads of three match sticks, and a 22-caliber bullet, all neatly wrapped in a small piece of waxed paper. I placed it in my wallet, and for at least two weeks afterwards either Estrelita or Marcelina would inquire if I had it with me whenever I left the house.

This was not my first experience with such beliefs in the supernatural. When I was a youngster living in Baguio City, our houseboy Felipe Valdez, an Ilocano from La Union Province, would occasionally invite me to his home for lunch. Once he also invited my good friend to come along. Before lunch, Joe and I played in the stream that flowed by Felipe's house. Suddenly, a woman screamed at us to get out of the streambed: "There's a ghost in amongst the boulders. I saw him last week. He has no head. He'll make you become sick and die! Get out! Get out now!" I was terrified and so was Joe. What frightened me was the complete conviction in her voice. For weeks afterwards I thought I might be dying. I couldn't confide my fear to my parents because they would have scoffed, "The woman was only teasing." But I knew she wasn't. I couldn't confide my fear to Felipe. I dreaded he would confirm it. To that woman the ghost was a real, visible, and threatening presence.

When the Spanish colonized the Philippines in the sixteenth century, Roman Catholic priests commenced missionary activities among the lowland peoples such as the Ilocanos, and these peoples quickly became Christianized. They were baptized, married, and buried in the church, but they did not altogether give up their traditional beliefs in the supernatural, perhaps because these beliefs help explain illness and misfortune. Catholicism enlarged rather than modified the Ilocano belief system. This is evident in the story that Alberto Ruiz told me of how he became an ambulario, a healer. Alberto, in his early fifties, is married and has several children, one of whom lives and works in Honolulu. This child, a daughter, plans to bring her parents to Hawaii as soon as she obtains citizenship. Alberto also has a son serving in the merchant marine.

Twenty years ago, Alberto says, when he and his wife were just starting a family, he became involved in a gambling ring in Bawang and began to lose a good deal of money. To break his ties to the ring, his parents advised him to take his family to the town of Bacarra where he had relatives and there was some land for him to farm. He remained in Bacarra for three years before returning to Bawang. The third year, spirits began to visit him. The visits lasted for five months.

The spirits came to Alberto both when he was dreaming and when he was awake. Sometimes he could see them. Other times he could only hear their voices. The visits caused him much anxiety, and he had a very difficult time sleeping during this period. He was first visited by ghosts who flew about his house at night. The ghosts were frightening in their appearance—only their heads had flesh; their arms and legs were bare. Next came a ravishingly beautiful woman with a fair complexion and long, curly blonde hair that fell to her shoulders. She was a *kastila,* of Spanish origin. For a month she visited Alberto daily and each time she insisted he marry her. If he didn't, she said, he would die. Alberto refused. He was already married, he replied, and he had responsibilities to his family. Further, she was a woman of great wealth, and he was a poor man. Marriage to her would be inconceivable.

The beautiful woman stopped visiting Alberto. In her place came her father, a dwarf with a long white beard. He demanded that Alberto marry his daughter, but Alberto refused. In subsequent months, Alberto was visited in turn by the woman's mother, who had a beautiful face like her daughter but no flesh on her body, and her brother, a young dwarf, both of whom made the same request and predicted the same dire consequences if Alberto continued to refuse. His fifth visitor was a huge, hideous creature with sunken eyes as big as fists. His message was the same, but it had a twist: if Alberto didn't agree to the marriage, not only would he die—but so would the beautiful woman. "You must marry to stay alive," the creature said, "and if you do, you'll have the power to cure people of their illnesses." Alberto finally, reluctantly, agreed. Then to his surprise the creature told him that he would not have to go through with the marriage. The spirits were satisfied with his willingness to become a healer.

That night the beautiful woman returned and took Alberto for a long walk, leading him along a path through the forest, always keeping about ten feet ahead of him. In the distance the path appeared to be strewn with thorns, but the thorns disappeared miraculously at their approach. Alberto recalls that he felt he was in paradise because he could hear birds singing sweetly everywhere. As the two continued through the forest, the beautiful woman pointed to twelve different plants and instructed Alberto in how to use them in his healing.

Finally, they came to a clearing and two giants appeared before them. One looked like the Virgin Mary and the other like Jesus Christ. Each wore a crucifix about its neck. The two giants performed a mass. Although he could not see them, Alberto sensed the presence of many spirits in attendance. During the mass, the beautiful woman touched Alberto on the shoulder and told him that now he possessed the gift of healing. "Return to your house, compadre," she said, "and help people." Alberto instantly found himself at home, miles from where the beautiful woman had taken him in the forest.

The very next day a voice told Alberto there was a gravely ill woman in a neighboring village and that he should go and heal her. Alberto departed for the village, walking along a path that led by the river. At the river he saw a man, who invited Alberto to his house. He told Alberto that his wife was ill. He said that a doctor (trained in Western medicine) had visited his wife recently but had been unable to cure her. Alberto offered to try, and the man agreed. Once at the house, Alberto instructed the husband to gather a certain type of grass. This Alberto boiled in water. He annointed the woman's body with the water, and mixed some of it with basi for her to drink. She recovered very quickly.

Then a few days later the same voice told him there was a young woman ill in Laoag and he was to cure her. The voice also told Alberto what the woman's house looked like so he would recognize it when he got to the city. The following day he and some friends went to Laoag to see a movie. On their way to the theater, they became thirsty and stopped at a house to request a drink. Alberto realized it was the one described to him by the voice. "Is anyone here ill?" Alberto asked a man who appeared at the doorway.

"Yes," the man replied, "my daughter." He said that for the past six months she had been suffering from menstrual problems. Alberto asked if he could try to cure her. The father agreed. Alberto instructed the father to pull up a particular bush, roots and all. Alberto stripped the bush of its leaves and put some of its roots and branches into a pot of water to boil. He also took a piece of root and placed it on the girl's head. The girl said she could feel power from the root flow through her body. Alberto rubbed her body with water from the pot and mixed some of it with basi for her to drink. Two days later she had fully recovered.

Alberto did not lose his healing ability even after moving back to Bawang with his family. But he has never again been visited by the beautiful woman, although from time to time a ghost swirls about his house at night, frightening his wife and children. Once, the family was having a midday meal when the head of a huge snake appeared in a window as if it were looking for something—or someone. Alberto said he began to pray to the Lord to deliver them from what was certainly an evil spirit. The snake's head began to disappear when Alberto started to pray.

Alberto's wife told me that just before her daughter and son-in-law left for Hawaii a few years before (the two lived with the

Ruizes), the daughter was awakened by the voice of an old, old woman who told her to go to where the paths met in the hills behind the house and, once there, reach into a large cauldron that would appear before her and draw out some money. But the daughter refused to go because she was afraid. It was a moonless night, and she had no one to accompany her to the crossroads. The old woman woke the daughter up three times and insisted that she go to the crossroads and collect money from the cauldron. Each time the daughter refused. Someone in the village had died recently; she felt it would be foolhardy to venture forth at night because she might meet the deceased's ghost. Yes, the old woman replied, there would be many ghosts and snakes at the site but none of them would harm her. She should not fear but have courage. When she returned home with the money, she should wake her husband and tell him to go to the cauldron. There he would reach in and find gold. The daughter, however, refused to go: the promise of wealth was fraught with too much danger.

Alberto's wife also told me that the spirits often come to visit her husband. She never sees them herself but she does hear voices around the house when they are present. The spirits come from distant Mount Mawakwakar, and they take Alberto to the mountain in a sailboat that floats in the air. There, they show him plants to use in his healing, and they feast on human flesh, inviting Alberto to join them. He refuses for fear of losing his healing power and his sanity. Cassandra Valdez, Alberto's wife pointed out, was once a powerful ambulario, but she had obviously eaten human flesh on a similar visit to Mount Mawakwakar and was now deranged as a consequence.

According to Alberto Ruiz, the spirits that reside on Mount Mawakwakar were created by God at the same time he created man. The spirits can be either malevolent or benevolent. They can take many shapes and forms, becoming visible or invisible at will. The spirits like the mountain because it is heavily forested. The forests teem with wildlife, and Alberto suspects that many wild creatures there are simply spirits manifesting themselves in natural forms.

Where do the spirits obtain the human flesh for the meals they offer their earthly guests at Mount Mawakwakar? Alberto says it is from humans they kill who stray too near their hiding places. Sev-

eral years ago, Alberto recalled, a villager climbed a tree in an isolated section of Bawang. The spirits killed him by making him slip
from the tree, and he died in the fall. When villagers found him,
they noticed to their horror that his liver had been sliced from his
body. Imelda Gomez, who rejected a call by the spirits to become a
healer, told me a similar story. The spirits offered her a meal of
human flesh that she believes may have been the liver of a girl killed
upriver a few days earlier. The girl's disemboweled body had been
found in a tree.

The spirits' recruitment of villagers to become ambularios is public knowledge. These individuals behave erratically for a period
lasting from weeks to several months. Some refuse to accept their
calling for one reason or another and return to their typical patterns
of behavior. Others accept their calling and become healers. Healing does not, however, become their full-time occupation; they
maintain their roles as farmers and garlic traders. The healers peri-
odically receive visits from powerful and dangerous spirits. A few
consume meals of human flesh offered to them by the spirits and
become mad, living proof of the spirits' incredible power.

Villagers believe that the spirits also recruit individuals to
become witches, but this recruitment is covert. Witches agree to
practice their craft in order to avoid being killed themselves by the
spirits. When witches die—and die they must—villagers wonder
whether the spirits have reclaimed their malevolent power or
whether the witches have instructed a friend or relative in their
craft.

One is never sure who is a witch until the evidence begins to
accumulate. In the last few years, most villagers in Bawang have
come to believe that Amparo Estacio is a witch. A grandmother in
her early sixties and a successful garlic trader, Amparo is suspected
of having recently caused three deaths in the village, the first that of
Fabian Pecua.

Fabian, a farmer, became very ill after attending a wedding feast
and died three weeks later. His wife Gloria, a nurse at the hospital
in Simbaan, told villagers that she was sure his death had been
caused by a witch—most likely Amparo, whom she had seen hand-
ing Fabian a plate of food at the feast. Furthermore, she had found
splinters of wood in his body when she prepared it for burial—sure
evidence that his death had been caused by a witch. Witches have

the power to kill by implanting foreign objects in their victims' flesh.

Amparo's next supposed victims were Margarita and her husband Florencio, both garlic traders. In the course of the trading season they had made some unfortunate buying and selling decisions and at the end of the season could not repay a loan from Amparo. Amparo was annoyed; she wanted the money to pay her own creditors. Margarita and Florencio also owed money to other villagers, but their largest debt was to Amparo. Shortly after the garlic season ended, Margarita and Florencio fell ill. Each suffered a painful and unsightly swelling in their stomach. Relatives took them to the hospital in Simbaan where Florencio died within three days. The fact that the doctors had been unable to save his life was proof to his relatives that his illness had been caused by a witch. The doctors could do nothing for Margarita, so her relatives brought her back to Bawang. There they decided to consult an ambulario from the neighboring province of Ilocos Sur to see what he would say about Margarita's illness. They told the ambulario that they suspected a witch had caused her illness and Florencio's death. They expressed a similar concern to municipal officials in Simbaan, whom they asked to be present when the ambulario visited Margarita.

During his visit, the ambulario put Margarita into a trance and asked her if a witch had caused her and Florencio's illness. Margarita replied in the affirmative. The ambulario then asked Margarita who the witch was. Margarita's voice suddenly changed: it was no longer her own. The voice belonged to Amparo Estacio, and it sounded exceedingly boastful. Yes, she had made Margarita and Florencio ill, and she had made other villagers ill, too—Tony, Marcita, Luis, among others. The voice suddenly stopped. Margarita lapsed into a coma and died two days later, never regaining consciousness.

Within a week the municipal authorities who had witnessed this incident summoned Amparo to Simbaan and told her to bring her malevolent activities to an end. Villagers in Bawang were angry with her, they said, and she would be wise to keep her distance from them for the time being, as best she could. Amparo denied being a witch, but she remained in or about her house, fearing retaliation. Her shunning of normal social activities, of course, further convinced villagers she was a witch.

Clearly, there is tension in the village, created, it is believed, by the interference of evil spirits in human affairs. Through those they pick to be witches, they inflict illness and even death. Other spirits seek to counteract this malevolence by selecting individuals like Alberto Ruiz and bestowing upon them miraculous healing powers. The healers are not always successful: sometimes clients come to them too late for their power to be effective or do not follow their advice to the letter. And sometimes the malevolence is simply too great for the healers to counteract. In these situations, friends and relatives of the victim sometimes take the matter into their own hands and kill or drive away the suspected source of the malevolence. Virginia Solano was killed by a relative of her supposed victim. The fact that no one other than her own children attended her funeral indicates that Virginia's fellow villagers did not think the killing unjust. Amparo Estacio's life was in danger for the same reason. She had to curb her power if she could, or perhaps share a similar fate.

Not all tension within Bawang can be attributed to the interference of evil spirits in human affairs. Sometimes its source can be quite ordinary. At the going away party for the Castros in 1974, Diony Bautista, the village captain, accused Maximo Espiritu of stealing some of his garlic. Insulted, Maximo struck Diony over the head with a beer bottle. The bottle broke and cut Diony, making him bleed profusely. Afraid Diony would seek revenge, Maximo would relate even to the chief of police in Simbaan how he believed Diony would one day try to kill him.

Berto Castro happened to remind me of this incident and other social tensions when I stopped by his house one afternoon for a visit. Sitting on his front porch smoking a cigarette, Berto immediately launched into what had evidently become his favorite gripe. "I don't go down to the highway anymore because too many young men ask me to buy cigarettes for them. I have to save my money for myself, you know." I chuckled. In 1973, Berto had just received his first veteran's pension check. At that time he had prided himself on his generosity, in contrast to all the retirees receiving social security benefits, whom he considered to be exceptionally selfish. While we were chatting, Polycarpio Ramirez drove by in his jeep, taking his wife and son for some shopping in Simbaan. "That man was always stingy," commented Berto. "Even when he was in America he was tight. He has no friends. Does he ever offer rides to anyone in the village?" Berto asked.

"Not that I've noticed," I replied.

"That's right. He never does."

Was Berto aware, I wondered, that his behavior seemed to be assuming a similar character? His involvement in village affairs was certainly less noticeable in 1975 than it had been two years before.

Many of the young men Berto was referring to were the sons of emigrants, all young, all married, and all, like my host Raphael, very envious of their parents and their single siblings who had emigrated. If the fourth preference opened, they too would emigrate. In the meantime, they assumed rather peculiar roles in the village. As the sons of emigrants and possible emigrants one day themselves, they felt that tilling the land was unbefitting their status. Most could afford to hire poorer villagers to farm their land for them. (Those who couldn't had wives who reluctantly shouldered the task.) They spent their time drinking and gambling, and none had a father or mother present to see to it that they did otherwise. For example, Berto told me that his neighbor Tranquilino Burgos owed a considerable sum to the local bank in Simbaan. He was able to qualify for a farm improvement loan but used the money instead for gambling.

"Perhaps," I suggested lamely, "his father will send him money from Hawaii to repay the loan." "No he won't," said Berto. "He's too disgusted with Tranquilino for being a good-for-nothing."

Included in this group of young men was Diony Bautista, who was married to the daughter of an emigrant. He farmed a few pieces of land belonging to his father-in-law on Guam and also a piece of land belonging to a spinster aunt who shared his household. Like Tranquilino, Diony had borrowed money from the local bank and used it for gambling. Every now and then, Diony and his friends brought prostitutes to the village. They set them up in business in a vacant shack by the river.

"Diony's no good," continued Berto, "and I tell Tranquilino to stay away from him, or he'll get in real trouble. Do you know about the fight Diony had with Maximo?"

"Yes," I replied.

"Well, I'm sure that isn't over yet."

I left Berto and went home to prepare for a week's visit to Manila. When I returned to Bawang from Manila, my host Raphael greeted me at the roadside. He seemed unusually excited, as if he had a momentous piece of news to share.

"Did anything happen, Raphael, while I was gone?"

"A murder! Maximo Espiritu was murdered."

"What?" My tone suggested disbelief.

"Yes! Wednesday night. At the river. He was shot twenty-two times in the chest and armpits. He was stabbed eight times in the back with a knife—and his head was cut off."

Rogelio Estacio and Crispin Tolentino had found Maximo's dismembered body Thursday morning when they went to the river to fish. Rogelio noticed Maximo's hat, shoes, and bolo lying on the riverbank and thought it odd that Maximo was nowhere in sight. Crispin was walking a few meters ahead of Rogelio. He stopped suddenly and called to Rogelio in a horror-filled voice. There before him lay Maximo's body in a still, discolored pool. A few feet away on a stretch of sand was his head. The stench was awful and flies danced in ferocious glee.

The men ran back to Bawang to notify Maximo's family and the municipal police in Simbaan. The police summoned criminal investigators in the Philippine Constabulary from Laoag. The investigators took pictures of Maximo's remains as they had been found at the river. Then villagers put Maximo's head in a basket and carried it with the body to his house. There a Simbaan mortician sewed the head to the body.

The funeral was held two days later when Maximo's daughters arrived from Bulacan in Central Luzon where they traded in garlic. Few visited the mourning family in the interval. Despite the fact that Maximo's body had been embalmed, the stench was foul and permeated the house and its environs. Visitors were fortunate: they could leave. Maximo's wife and children could not. Furthermore, they were required by custom to mourn and keen over the open casket whenever a visitor was present.

Who committed the murder? No one knew for sure, but everyone suspected Diony Bautista because of his long-standing grudge with Maximo. Manuel Valdez, a villager who taught at the Simbaan elementary school, told me that on Wednesday evening—the night of the murder—he was playing his guitar at the New Popular

Store when Pascual Gomez passed by on his way to the river to fish. Pascual asked Manuel if Maximo had preceded him. No, Manuel replied, he hadn't seen Maximo. Having already waited for him at his house, Pascual decided to go ahead. Maximo knew the spot where Pascual planned to fish; surely he would follow shortly.

While he was at the store, Manuel did not see Maximo go to the river. But while he was playing his guitar, a group of four men gathered at the store: Diony Bautista, Tranquilino Burgos, Bonifacio Tolentino, and Gregorio Gomez. Like Tranquilino, Bonifacio was the son of emigrants in Hawaii. Gregorio was the son of Pascual, who had gone to the river to fish. The four men started to drink and sing songs, and after a while they decided to serenade in Balay Kayu, a cluster of homes south of the village. To get there they followed a trail along the river.

Officials suspected the four men of committing the murder. Constabulary investigators took them to Laoag Thursday afternoon for questioning and to administer paraffin tests to see if any had recently fired a pistol.

Pascual told villagers that Maximo was not at the river when he arrived. He set his fish traps anyway, hoping that Maximo would soon follow. When Pascual decided Maximo was not going to show up, he went to a shack near his rice fields to sleep. The shack was located quite a distance from where he had been fishing—and where Maximo's remains were found.

Some villagers claimed to have heard gunshots at midnight, and perhaps these were the shots that killed Maximo. However, Jésus Burgos, a retiree whose house was near Maximo's, insisted that he saw and spoke with Maximo at four o'clock in the morning. Jésus happened to be up because he was waiting for the pan-de-sal vendor from Simbaan, who delivered his wares early in the morning. In fact, said Jésus, he was standing on his porch when Maximo walked by with his fish traps, apparently on his way to the river. The two called greetings to each other. However, Maximo's wife said that he did not spend the night at home, that he left the house at five o'clock Wednesday afternoon to join Pascual.

Villagers were exceptionally alarmed by the murder. Some made their first attempt to speak with me in English to discuss the event (which, in retrospect, does not say much for what they thought of my Ilocano). Some even believed that "outsiders" may have been responsible for the murder rather than the village captain and his friends. In fact, a rumor spread quickly that six convicts had escaped from a prison in Laoag and had made their way south the day before the murder. Thus, when Berto called a meeting to organize a schedule and system of village guards, many attended. Each section of the village (six in all) agreed to post four guards throughout the night. Household heads would take turns assuming guard duty and the system would remain in effect until the crime was solved. The only household head to protest was retiree Polycarpio Ramiriz, who insisted that he, unlike the others, was not obliged to stand guard duty because he was an American citizen. In fact, he pointed out, it was the duty of Bawang villagers to guard him. Ricardo Valdez, one of the most respected men in the village and Diony's opponent in the last election, told Polycarpio that if he didn't want to meet his obligations as a resident of the village, he was quite welcome to return to California.

According to Raphael, the gun that was likely used to kill Maximo had once been owned by a Philippine Constabulary soldier, who sold it to Diony Bautista just two weeks prior to the murder. The murder weapon itself had not yet been found, but tests conducted by the criminal investigators in Laoag indicated that the bullets removed from Maximo's body could have been fired from this gun. Diony insisted that he sold the gun to someone else before the murder, but he didn't say to whom.

Two days after I got back from Manila I went to Simbaan to check my census data against church records. On my way I met Berto, who looked tired and concerned. He said, with a trace of disgust in his voice, that the suspects were "smiling" because they were home free. "But," Berto concluded, "the investigation isn't over yet, and the suspects will learn that 'crime doesn't pay.'" As he spoke, Diony Bautista rested on a bench near the New Popular Store. His wife sat nearby, and Nicomedes Valdez picked lice from her hair. I noticed later, upon my return from Simbaan, that Diony's wife accompanied him to the river to cut grass to feed his livestock, perhaps in the belief that he was safe from reprisals in her presence.

On each of the following three days constabulary officers came to Bawang to pick up suspects and take them to Laoag for questioning. In addition to taking in Diony Bautista, Tranquilino Burgos, Bonifacio Tolentino, and Gregorio Gomez, they also picked up Pascual, who was supposed to have been with Maximo the night of the murder, and, for an unexplained reason, Diony's brother Pablo. Pablo cried and wept as he was ordered into the constabulary jeep. Villagers said this was a sure sign that he was guilty. But perhaps Pablo had other concerns, such as the fear of having to deal with the powerful constabulary officers who were rumored to have tortured Bonifacio Tolentino. When Bonifacio was picked up with the other three suspects the day after the murder, constabulary officers hit him several times in the stomach and burned his fingers badly with the heated paraffin. All the suspects were released after questioning except Diony.

On the fourth day, the officers returned to Bawang to pick up Pascual for a second round of questioning. This terrified him. He vomited and shook violently as he climbed into the constabulary jeep. He told his sons and daughters who had accompanied him to the roadside that they would never see him again. In Laoag the constabulary officers questioned Pascual about the murder until Pascual became so ill with shaking and vomiting he could no longer pay heed. The officers took him to a nearby hospital where he died. Villagers believe that Pascual may have swallowed rat poison when he went into his house, ostensibly to change his shirt, before leaving with the officers for Laoag. Others say he probably drank a whole bottle of gin. Either would account for his shaking and vomiting. Doctors at the hospital say Pascual died of a stroke.

Word spread quickly in the village that before he died Pascual had signed an affadavit stating that he had witnessed Maximo's murder and naming the murderer. During his first interview, Pascual had reportedly been given a lie detector test, and the results of the test indicated that Pascual had been present when the murder was committed. The officers had brought him back to Laoag a second time to persuade him to name the murderer. This would account for Pascual's great stress. He knew what he was going to be asked, and he feared the consequences of either providing or not providing an answer. Villagers were convinced of this rumor's authenticity. Pascual Gomez, they said, would never have spent the night in the shack by his rice fields if he had not had a companion. Presumably, the murderer and his accomplices told Pascual that they would spare his life if he swore never to identify them. He would be killed in retaliation if he did. Since the constabulary detained only Diony Bautista, villagers assumed that Pascual did not reveal who Diony's accomplices were. (Pascual's son Gregorio was believed to be one of them.)

In the days to come, the constabulary picked up more men for questioning, but they were all released. Diony Bautista was the only one who continued to be detained. He was still in prison when I left the village for Hawaii two months later. Marcelina told me that she heard he had uncontrollable fits of shaking in the provincial jail where he was held. He was scared, she said, that the constabulary soldiers would cut off his head as a punishment to fit his crime. The mayor of Simbaan appointed Berto Castro village captain, and Berto, in contrast to the months before the murder, spent much of his time again at the New Popular Store, gathering and disseminating gossip and news. In early November the rice harvest started and, perhaps as a consequence, the village guard system slowly collapsed. Tired from more than a full day's work in the fields, men slept at their guard stations. Raphael hired Nicomedes Valdez to assume his guard duty. Those who could afford it also hired substitutes to take their places.

Most villagers believed that Diony Bautista was guilty of the murder, although no formal charges had yet been brought in the case. His imprisonment was adequate proof. Surely others had been involved in the murder, but it now appeared doubtful if any of them would be jailed unless Diony confessed to the crime and named his accomplices. In any case, villagers were relieved that Diony was no longer the village captain. In the last election he had bullied himself into office by threatening his opponent, Ricardo Valdez, into withdrawing from the race just a few days before the election. Diony was neither well liked nor a capable leader. In 1974 he had raped the maid of a Bawang retiree. He hid from municipal authorities for a month until he was apprehended and fined, but not jailed, for his deed. He had also borrowed money from several individuals in the village and appropriated a thousand pesos of village funds for his own use. Now, when it became apparent that he

was not going to be released from prison anytime soon, villagers to
whom he owed money approached his wife for repayment. She had
nothing to offer them.

One morning several weeks after the murder, as I was typing up
notes, I heard screams coming from a house near the national highway. These were not screams of joy for a returning Hawaiiano but
rather screams of grief. I learned later that Roberta Estacio had just
received the news that her husband Buenaventura had died of a
stroke in Sanchez, Cagayan, 150 kilometers north of Bawang.
Until losing his arm in a bus accident two years before, Buenaventura had worked for a national bus company as a conductor. He
served on the route between Laoag and Sanchez. In Sanchez he had
a common-law wife who bore him four children (he had seven by
his wife in Bawang). Although he received compensation from the
company for his accident, Buenaventura was deeply in debt and
unemployed. He was thirty-eight when he died.

Untimely as his death was, it permitted villagers upset by Maximo's murder and Pascual's possible suicide to demonstrate their
neighborliness and generosity. Filomena Corpuz loaned Roberta
Estacio her minibus and driver so that she and her father-in-law
could travel to Sanchez and claim Buenaventura's body. Raphael
went with Bejamen Corpuz, Filomena's husband, to San Nicholas
to purchase cement blocks for Buenaventura's tomb.

Villagers who attended Buenaventura's funeral—and there were
many because he was a popular man—gave Roberta a total of ₱700
to help cover its cost. Members of the sociedad contributed another
₱300. Buenaventura's common-law wife, who remained in Sanchez, paid for the coffin, the embalmment, and in addition contributed ₱300. Roberta had the family's pig butchered and cooked to
feed the many guests.

About three hundred villagers, myself included, walked in the
funeral procession to Simbaan. Only a fraction, however, actually
attended the service at the Roman Catholic church, preferring, as I
did, to sit under a shade tree in the plaza, waiting for the service to
end and the procession to continue on to the cemetery.

The ceremony at the cemetery was brief. Buenaventura's friends
opened the casket so his wife and children could make their last
farewell. The corpse was a ghastly gray, and the children ap-

proached their father's lifeless body rather reluctantly. As the coffin was closed and shoved into the tomb, Rogelio Estacio, who had discovered Maximo's headless body at the river, called out jokingly —referring to Buenaventura's career as a conductor: "Don't forget, Buenaventura, to make reservations for the rest of us!"

I was to learn after my return to Hawaii that one of the first villagers Buenaventura made a reservation for was Diony Bautista. Diony died of a stroke in the provincial jail in Laoag, less than six months after Maximo's murder.

Epilogue:
Leave-Taking

One afternoon, near the end of my second field trip, I noticed a sign posted on a board near the New Popular Store with the message that a reception sponsored by the Bawang Progressive Club would be held that evening for Arturo Magbaleta. Arturo was being "ordered" to Guam by his son and daughter-in-law. At fifty-five years of age, Arturo, if lucky, would be able to work for ten years before retiring and becoming eligible for social security benefits. Would he return to Bawang for his retirement? The prospect was doubtful, as Arturo would certainly send for his two unmarried children and his wife to join him on Guam. Once reunited there with his family, he and his wife would find it difficult to leave behind their children and grandchildren.

Later, while I was eating dinner with the Solanos, my friend Manuel Valdez came by to tell me that the reception for Arturo would be held at Ricardo Valdez' house. When we finished eating, Raphael and I walked to Ricardo's house where we found the reception well underway. Few people were in attendance—just officials of the club, village counselors, and other influential leaders. Arturo was a village counselor himself and a past officer of the club. Ricardo's wife served noodles, bread, and coffee.

Soon after we arrived, informal chatting ceased, and almost everyone present stood in turn to tell Arturo that they were sad to see him leave, that they hoped he would not forget Bawang, and that he would return to the village to retire. Ricardo reminded Arturo, a diligent and skilled farmer, that on Guam he would not be able to plow or plant rice. Berto evoked laughter when he said that everyone in the village would rush to the road to greet Arturo upon his return to Bawang—and he'd better have plenty of Lucky Strikes and Camels to give them as gifts. Arturo, the last to speak, came close to tears when he thanked his friends for what they had said. He told them that he would not forget Bawang, and he hoped that they did not think badly of him for leaving. He asked that village counselors assume his responsibilities as president of the Abagatan irrigation society and find a means to drain excess water from the fields during the monsoon season so two crops of rice could be planted each year instead of just one. Berto nodded and said that he and his fellow counselors would try to make sure this was accomplished. Arturo stopped speaking and silently embraced each of his friends. The gathering broke up, and everyone went home.

Arturo left for Manila the next day. Many relatives went to the airport to bid him farewell. As he got on the bus in front of the New Popular Store, perhaps he glanced at the Simbaan River and remembered how, as a child, he would follow the young men who left for Hawaii to the river's edge. In the 1920s the national highway had not yet been built and HSPA recruits had to walk to Simbaan to meet the recruiters. At the river the young men stripped. Each tied his clothes and sandals into a bundle, placed it on his head, and stepped into the smooth current. The water came as high as their chests. Reaching the opposite bank, the young men stood in the sun to dry before dressing and continuing on to Simbaan. Arturo could still remember how their strong, naked bodies glistened in the sunlight.

The boy Arturo would wade into the river's shallows and watch the recruits cross. Among them once were his older brother and many of his brother's friends. He looked forward to the day he could go to Hawaii himself, but by the time he was old enough, his father had persuaded him to stay in Bawang and farm his land. Arturo married and established a family. His brother never returned from Hawaii, although many of his brother's friends did, including Enrique Cruz and Berto Castro. As the years passed, he lost interest in going abroad himself. But then his son married the daughter of an emigrant and now he was on his way to join them. Initially, Arturo had been reluctant to emigrate, but his unmarried children in Bawang urged him to. They told him that he would be able to send for them after he became a U.S. citizen. They did not want to remain in Bawang farming his land. Their bridge to the future was Arturo.

Before I left Bawang myself, I purchased a large pig and invited all the villagers and municipal officials who had assisted me with my research to a feast, which my hosts, Raphael and Estrelita, and their friends prepared. I also rented a slide projector and showed villagers pictures I had taken of them. The show was a big success, and they insisted on a repeat performance the next night. I was happy to oblige. Afterwards many villagers asked me to take letters to their relatives in Hawaii, to which I agreed. The total came close to a hundred. It took me a week to distribute them after I arrived in Honolulu.

Raphael, Estrelita, and Marcelina went to Manila to see me off at the airport. Marcelina told me that Doting had wanted to come too, but that Estrelita had asked her to remain behind to take care of the children. I wondered how well Doting was handling Raphael and Estrelita's sometimes rambunctious offspring, knowing that their occasional tantrums annoyed her greatly.

As I boarded the plane, neither Raphael nor Estrelita had to tell me how much they wished they were going to Hawaii themselves. Because the fourth preference was closed, they were sure they would never be able to emigrate. But two years later in 1977 the fourth and fifth preferences opened, and Raphael was able to persuade his father Donato to send for him and Estrelita. Marcelina agreed to care for Raphael and Estrelita's sons until they could afford to send for them—despite the fact that her daughter in California wanted her to emigrate.

In Honolulu, Raphael and Estrelita took up residence with Donato and his second wife and within days found employment, Raphael in a tuna packing company and Estrelita as a seamstress. Since immigrating to Hawaii, Raphael and Estrelita have returned to Bawang for a vacation and have sent for their sons to join them. In 1986 they purchased a home in Waipahu and are now in the process of ordering Marcelina to Hawaii. Estrelita writes that she is expected to arrive any day.

Forty-two years ago, Marcelina's former husband Donato went to Hawaii in the last HSPA recruitment, leaving her in Bawang with two young children to raise. At the age of sixty-five, after seeing first her husband, then her children and grandchildren emigrate, she is on her way to Hawaii herself. She will be greeted warmly.

Left behind is the spinster aunt Doting, the only member of the family who chose to remain in Bawang.

INDEX

abal-abal, 33–35
ambulario, 51, 71–72, 75–76, 79, 80
an-annong, 51
anib, 50, 74

basi, 28, 48, 49, 77
Bawang Progressive Club, 62, 67, 69–70, 91

Crusaders' Church of Christ, 31

Depression, the, 4, 13, 20, 22
divorce, 41, 54, 60
dowry, 16, 24, 25, 48–49, 56

emigrants, 36–37, 38–39, 55, 57, 62; in California, 4, 13, 37, 70; in Guam, 4, 37; in Hawaii, 4, 37–39, 70, 74; sons of, 82; wives of, 57, 60 (*see also* divorce). *See also* retirees; returned emigrants
emigration, 1, 3, 5, 35–37, 55, 56, 60
entrepreneurship, 5, 55, 60–61. *See also* garlic trading
evil spirits. *See* supernatural beliefs

fiesta, 4, 5, 19, 39, 61, 62, 65, 67–70

garlic trading, 4, 5, 55, 57–60
ghosts. *See* supernatural beliefs

Hawaii Sugar Planters' Association (HSPA), 16, 36, 38, 40, 68, 92, 93

Ilocos region, 1, 2, 4, 16
inheritance, 16

kakawate, 33–34, 51

landlord/tenant relationship, 55–57
Ligot, Commissioner, 12–13

Manlapit, Pablo, 12
May–December marriages, 17, 24, 28
merchant marine, 4, 18, 44–45, 61

palay, 40
pamisa, 14, 31, 39
patron/client tie, 55, 56
Philippine Constabulary, 62, 66, 83, 84, 85, 86, 87
plantation life in Hawaii: cockfighting, 11, 18, 21; gardens, 10; *hopai-ko,* 9; leisure activities, 10–11; living arrangements, 8, 9, 11; *luna,* 8–9, 14; recruitment for, 7, 16; retirement benefits, 17, 18; ritual kinship, 12; Simbaan-Santos Association, 12, 68–69; strikes, 12–13; sudden death syndrome, 12; unionization, 17; work schedule, 8

remittances, 10, 11, 37, 56, 57, 60, 69
retirees, 17, 18, 22, 23, 24, 27, 29, 56–57, 60, 61, 81. *See also* May–December marriages; retirement homes
retirement homes, 3, 25, 29
returned emigrants, 3, 7, 17, 55, 56, 68. *See also* retirees
ritual kinship, 27, 56. *See also* plantation life in Hawaii: ritual kinship
Roman Catholicism, 75

sarabo, 39
Simbaan-Santos Association. *See* plantation life in Hawaii
social security, 17, 20, 34, 36, 54
sociedad, 68–70, 88
spinsters, 16, 17, 29
spirits. *See* supernatural beliefs
supernatural beliefs, 5, 50, 51, 71, 72, 73, 74–81. *See also ambulario; an-annong; anib;* Roman Catholicism

ABOUT THE AUTHOR

Philip Adam

Stephen Griffiths grew up in the Mountain Province of the Philippines where his father, an Episcopal minister, served as a missionary and educator. He graduated from Hobart College in 1968, where he earned a B.A. in English. As a Peace Corps volunteer in Malaysia from 1968 to 1970, Griffiths taught English at an elementary school on the small island of Pulau Perhentian, Trengganu State. He began graduate studies in anthropology at the University of Hawaii in 1971, earning an M.A. in 1974 and a Ph.D. in 1978.

The research on which this book is based was conducted during two field trips to the province of Ilocos Norte, both for eight months, one in 1973 and another in 1975. After teaching for four years in the University of Hawaii system, Griffiths moved to San Francisco in 1981 to work for the Sierra Club. His current book project is a manuscript about his parents' experience in the Philippines.

Production Notes

This book was designed by Roger Eggers.
Composition and paging were done on the
Quadex Composing System and typesetting
on the Compugraphic 8400 by the design
and production staff of University of
Hawaii Press.

The text typeface is Sabon and the
display typeface is Caslon Light.

Offset presswork and binding were done by
Vail-Ballou Press, Inc. Text paper is
Glatfelter Offset Vellum, basis 50.